# HOW TO KEEP AND
# GROW
## YOUR RETIREMENT
# ASSETS

## New Investment Strategies for a New Reality

DANIEL WILDERMUTH

Mc
Graw
Hill

New York   Chicago   San Francisco   Lisbon   London   Madrid   Mexico City
Milan   New Delhi   San Juan   Seoul   Singapore   Sydney   Toronto

The *McGraw·Hill* Companies

1  2  3  4  5  6  7  8  9  10    QFR/QFR    1  8  7  6  5  4  3  2

ISBN  978-0-07-180019-8
MHID      0-07-180019-0
e-ISBN  978-0-07-180020-4
e-MHID      0-07-180020-4

**Library of Congress Cataloging-in-Publication Data**
Wildermuth, Daniel.
   How to keep and grow your retirement assets : new investment strategies for a new reality / by Daniel Wildermuth.
      p. cm.
   ISBN-13: 978-0-07-180019-8 (alk. paper)
   ISBN-10: 0-07-180019-0 (alk. paper)
   1.  Retirement income—Planning.  2.  Portfolio management.  3.  Investments.
4.  Finance, Personal.  I.  Title.
   HG179.W532 2013
   332.024′0145—dc23                                                      2012036258

# Contents

# From the Author

Dear Reader,

Given today's volatility and complexity, successfully managing your finances if you are in or near retirement is more important than ever. Compared to just a decade ago, the amount of information, choices, possibilities, and potential problems is vastly greater. Issues such as income, growth, and risk of losses have always been important to anyone who is nearing or in retirement, and managing these challenges can be more difficult given today's volatile stock market, record low interest rates, and high probability of increasing inflation.

Fortunately, many of the same events that are generating today's challenges also create far more options and fantastic opportunities! In fact, today's investors enjoy unprecedented means to achieve financial success.

Before running through some explanations of possibilities, I'll acknowledge some challenges. The poor investment climate since the turn of the century may have tempted some people to limit their exposure to any risk, or even to abandon the world of investments altogether. It's been rough for many investors. Yet many, if not most, people who are nearing or in retirement have little choice but to keep their money working for them. Increasing life expectancies, greater expectations for retirement activities, ultra-low yields on safe or guaranteed investments, and higher future inflation expectations all make successful investing more important than ever.

Finding investment success may also appear elusive given the many problems constantly highlighted by journalists, politicians, pundits, and seemingly anyone with a platform from which to preach. The new millennium has already subjected investors to two severe stock market crashes, the 9/11 tragedy, European and U.S. debt problems, various bubbles and busts, corporate scandals, record low interest rates, vastly increased regulation, and dramatically increased volatility. The list of challenges is already long and will undoubtedly grow. For some investors, the future may not look much brighter, and some people have lowered their expectations for their personal finances and investments.

Yet, tremendous changes in financial markets are opening up many new opportunities, and the many problems over the past decade plus have also created a much more inviting investment climate. Just a few reasons for my optimism will help to explain this.

First, most investors continue to follow very traditional and dated investment strategies. They have not taken basic steps to shield themselves from the inevitable problems, nor have they positioned themselves to benefit from vastly expanded opportunities. Low interest rates and expected future increases in inflation further emphasize the limitations of traditional approaches, especially for investors who are in or near retirement.

These traditional and dated strategies contrast sharply with the more advanced approaches employed by college endowments, various institutions such as pension funds, and high-net-worth investors. These more sophisticated investors dramatically altered their investment strategies years ago and have generally enjoyed tremendous success since the turn of the century, while facing the same circumstances as individual investors. Investment strategies and even specific investments pursued by these more sophisticated investors are increasingly becoming available to individuals with portfolios of nearly any size. This factor alone offers tremendous potential for any investor to dramatically increase the likelihood of investment success and was the focus of my last book (*Wise Money: Minimize Your Volatility and Increase your Control*, McGraw-Hill, 2012).

Second, as of this writing, most assets with strong performance potential, such as stocks, real assets such as including real estate, and new debt instruments that are filling the void left by damaged credit markets, are priced below their historical averages. By this, I mean that it takes less money than is normally required to buy a given dollar of earnings capability, whether the dollar of profit comes from stocks, real estate, private equity, or various nontraditional debt instruments. When valuations—the price required to buy a given dollar of earnings—are low, future returns tend to be strong. This situation contrasts sharply with the circumstances in the late 1990s, when stock valuations hit record highs, setting the stage for terrible performance in the ensuing decade.

Valuations continually fluctuate over time, but they tend to move fairly slowly, so this opportunity is likely to remain available for years. Just as important, increased access to different investments probably means that investors will enjoy access to more types of assets that may have lower valuations and can offer greater growth potential. Depressed prices for many different potential investments are causing some of the current pessimism, but they are also likely to create great buying opportunities. And, when valuations are lower, investors tend to benefit from not only higher return expectations, but also lower likelihood of loss, since large price declines become less probable when valuations are already lower.

Third, the world is experiencing tremendous change and growth. Investors have new opportunities to benefit from the greatest and fastest wealth generation ever experienced by the planet. Many opportunities are continually arising in the United States as we find ways to serve other countries that are growing more rapidly than we are, and direct investments are also becoming much easier to find and access. It can be easy to miss the phenomenal increase in global prosperity given all the turmoil the United States has been experiencing.

Global growth continues to hit new highs. The microchip is changing the planet and accelerating growth and change in every industry in every country. More stable and pro-market-economy political systems across the globe are propelling a vast expansion in the number of countries growing at rates above 3 percent.

A generation or two ago, only a small minority of countries across the globe—about 25—enjoyed sustained economic growth. Now, only political or economic outliers are struggling in their self-imposed exile. Even Africa is joining the party. In the United States, energy prices are dropping and appear poised to remain at low levels, and this will provide the United States with cost advantages for decades. The United States is the fastest-growing oil and natural gas producer in the world, resulting in projections that the United States could become energy independent as early as 2020. In fact, the United States is bringing on so much new production that it could reach the almost unthinkable position of being a net exporter of crude oil, refined products, and natural gas.[1] There is a lot of good news for the future, even if it's not immediately obvious.

Lastly, resources for investors have expanded dramatically. These range from vastly greater information availability on the Internet to improved access to a wide range of financial professionals who can be readily screened via online background data checks. Investors have more resources, information, and choices than ever before to do it alone or find a competent financial professional to help them.

All these factors, and more, present an incredible opportunity for individual investors to participate in domestic and global growth. Yet the pace of change seems to ensure that volatility is here to stay and will probably increase. As a result, investment success in a rapidly changing economy is likely to require significant adjustments to traditional investment strategies. The investment world that your parents and grandparents traveled in is as dated as their rotary phone. Fortunately, I believe that nearly any investor who is willing to adjust his or her portfolio strategy and financial assumptions can easily make constructive changes that will make success more likely for multiple reasons.

This book seeks to provide investors with an investment road map that can help anyone keep and grow retirement assets in a very different world that offers unprecedented opportunity accompanied by a bewildering and increasingly faster pace of change. I discuss various straightforward investment strategies that can help investors navigate today's challenges and dramatically altered investment landscape.

While many of the strategies and approaches are based on sophisticated theory used by some of the world's most successful college endowments, institutions, and professional investors, I have converted these theories into simple, uncomplicated actions that I think you'll find highly interesting, easy to understand, and fun to implement.

In addition, I believe these strategies will help you control what can be the most dangerous and destructive factor in investing—your own emotions. A better approach should lessen the likelihood that fear and greed, characteristics that afflict us all, will drive detrimental actions. Instead, you can employ an improved investment strategy that can greatly increase your odds of reaching your definition of success while also making ongoing management and oversight emotionally easier.

Daniel Wildermuth

# 1

# Why Invest?

FOR SOME PEOPLE, AVOIDING FINANCIAL RISK IS POSSIBLE, AND could even be advisable. If you have a wonderful pension with a cost of living adjustment, or if you have a large portfolio and little need of additional future income, you may be able to avoid investing entirely. Other people have little need to increase the size of their portfolio and have no desire to grow their financial assets. I am guessing, however, that since you're reading this book, you aren't in this type of situation. Whether you need to or not, you want to invest your money, and you want to make wise investment decisions.

To put it simply, if you are like most people, you want to improve your financial situation. What this means to different people can vary tremendously, but the answers usually fall into a few general categories.

Most people want some combination of growth and income with an acceptable level of risk. If you are already retired, you are probably more interested in income and the safety of your principal. For people who are still adding to their portfolio before retirement, the focus may be more on growth.

Going a bit further, most investors are aware of the importance of maintaining their purchasing power, particularly in light of expectations that inflation will increase in the future. It may seem rational to take little risk, but inflation can quickly erode the value of assets that are in highly conservative savings vehicles and are earning little. Expectations and plans regarding a future lifestyle may require solid portfolio growth and income generation.

Some people place a lot of importance on providing for or helping the next generation. And many people derive a great deal of satisfaction from achieving a desired level of success with their investments.

Increasing life spans and increasingly active lifestyles also heighten the importance of taking care of your finances. If you're just retiring at around the age of 65, you probably need to plan for a 30-year time horizon. This differs dramatically from the 2-year life expectancy of the average 65-year-old when social security was created.

In addition, humans are wired to continually strive for more rather than settle for less. We may retrench and shore up our circumstances in the short run, but eventually, we push to better ourselves. And Americans seem particularly prone to striving to improve. It's part of our DNA.

Against this backdrop, the new millennium has frustrated countless investors. The dot-com collapse and then the financial meltdown destroyed a lot of portfolio value for many people and created an even greater need for future growth while reducing or eliminating financial cushions. Many people are wondering whether they should still be trying to invest, or whether more responsible management dictates taking much less risk or even avoiding most or all investments.

But you may be like so many other investors who are struggling to identify the best path forward or to adjust to different circumstances and opportunities. Striving for investment success seems responsible, and may also be desperately needed if you are to enjoy a planned lifestyle either now or during a future retirement. For many people, the route to success probably isn't as obvious as it seemed to be just a few short years ago. The poor performance of most traditional strategies in recent years has created much confusion for many investors.

Not surprisingly, many investors are not enthusiastic about jumping back into the same investments or strategies that disappointed them in the past. Individuals' limited success certainly highlights the potential problems with following dated and flawed strategies and investment plans.

This book will highlight many different ways to achieve financial success. Before jumping into solutions, however, I will start by covering problems with the various approaches taken by most individual investors. Understanding both the severity of the problem and its major causes should make it easier to adopt approaches that I believe are far more likely to result in predictable and comfortable success.

For instance, stocks struggled from 2000 to 2011, achieving an annual gain of only 0.55 percent.[1] Yet most investors did far worse than the stock market for various reasons ranging from fees to mismanagement. This isn't a problem that's unique to this time period, as it's been true for many decades.

Before I move onward, a little explanation will be helpful here. To illustrate and clarify different points throughout the book, various different data sources will be used. To simplify later sections, I'll explain some terms and data sources here rather than repeatedly providing the same details. When I mean something other than what's defined here, I'll be specific.

"U.S. stocks" and "the market" refer to the S&P 500, the capitalization-weighted index published in its current form since 1957 and widely available in a usable, standard format since 1926. This index tracks the prices of the 500 largest, most actively traded firms in the United States and is generally viewed as the most representative index of the U.S. stock market. "Capitalization-weighted" means that the components, or companies, that make up the index are weighted according to the total market value of their outstanding shares.

You may be surprised that I don't use the very common Dow Jones Industrial Average (DJIA). While the DJIA is certainly a solid and well-known index, most studies and academic work refer to the S&P 500, partly because it includes 500 stocks rather than the 30 in the DJIA. Using the broader S&P 500 is much easier because information is so much more widely available. All the data I use were supplied directly by Standard & Poor's, the owner and maintainer of this index.[2]

For foreign developed stock market performance, the MSCI EAFE Index is used. This index includes more than 6,000 stocks from 24 developed markets but excludes equities from the United States and Canada.[3] The acronym MSCI EAFE stands for Morgan Stanley Capital International Europe, Australasia, and Far East. Like the S&P 500, the index is market capitalization–weighted. All data were supplied by MSCI, the firm that owns and maintains the index.

Since 1988, MSCI has also maintained the standard benchmark for emerging markets, predictably named the MSCI Emerging Markets Index. Because emerging markets have grown and evolved considerably over the last few decades, this index has been much more fluid than most others. As of this writing, the index includes more than 2,700 securities in 21 countries that are currently classified as emerging market countries.[4] MSCI owns, maintains, and supplied the data for this index as well.

Price and yield performance for general bond returns are defined by the Barclays Capital U.S. Aggregate Bond Index, formerly known as the Lehman Aggregate Bond Index. After Lehman Brothers collapsed in April 2008, Barclays Capital bought the rights to this index from the defunct Lehman Brothers and now maintains it. This index provides a measure of the U.S. investment-grade bond market performance and includes U.S. government bonds, investment-grade corporate bonds, mortgage pass-through securities, and asset-backed securities publicly offered for sale in the United States All bond data were supplied directly by Barclays Capital, the new owner and maintainer of this index.

Now let's cover some of the shortcomings of some common strategies used by individual investors.

# Performance Problems

## How Bad Are They?

While different asset classes can struggle over time and usually do so occasionally, a more predictable trend seems to be the underperformance of individual investors relative to nearly everything else. Investors seem to have a sixth sense regarding how to inflict the most damage on their own finances.

They sell when they should buy, they readily adopt crazy strategies, and they use the wrong investment vehicles to gain exposure to particular asset classes. A few simple statistics from different time frames make the point clearly. These trends illustrate that this phenomenon is not just a new or an old problem. It's been here a long time, and it doesn't seem to be fading.

A great deal of research has been done on this subject, and studies routinely illustrate very similar patterns. DALBAR, Inc., is a well-known and respected financial research company that compiles and publishes various investor performance data. In a recent annual study, it reported the 20-year performance data ending in 2011 shown in Figure 2.1.[1]

**Figure 2.1**  2011 DALBAR QAIB Study (20 Years Ending December 31, 2011)

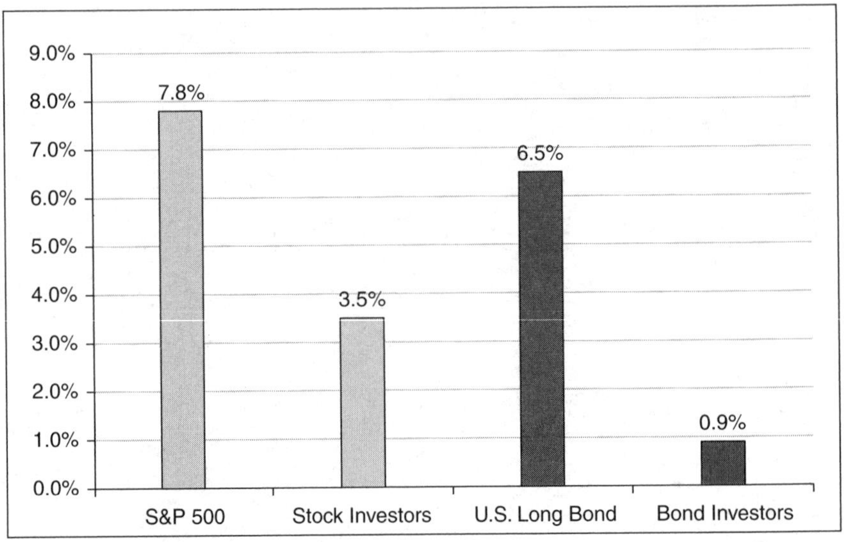

*Source:* DALBAR, Inc., "Quantitative Analysis," April 2012.

The spread of more than 4 percent between investors' performance and the indexes' performance is pretty dramatic and surpasses the amounts that could be attributed to fees.

Studies from older time frames show similar performance deficiencies. Another DALBAR study on the 17-year stock market boom from 1984 to 2000 revealed similar problems. The study reported that the average stock mutual fund grew at 14 percent per year.[2] However, the typical mutual fund investor earned only 5.3 percent per year. The difference is much greater than it appears because of compounding. Over the 17-year time period, an annual difference of 2.64 times (14 percent/5.3 percent) grows into nearly a fourfold difference. One dollar in the average mutual fund grew to about $9.25, while the average mutual fund investor saw his dollar grow to only about $2.40.[3]

The average investor managed to convert the returns of a fantastic bull market into mediocre performance that couldn't even keep pace with bonds.

**Figure 2.2**   One-Year Returns for 2011

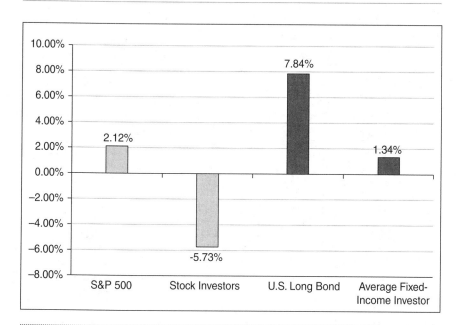

*Source:* DALBAR, Inc., "Quantitative Analysis," April 2012.

Looking at more recent numbers, investors don't appear to be improving.[4] The numbers in Figure 2.2 are so bad that they seem impossible to achieve without a sophisticated strategy that ensures terrible performance.

Unfortunately, other studies demonstrate the same patterns. Between 1998 and 2001, the Firsthand Technology Value Fund produced an impressive annualized return of 16 percent. Yet the average individual investor in this fund *lost* 31.6 percent over this time period.[5] The performance differences illustrate classic investor mismanagement. When the fund went down, investors sold, and after it went up, they bought, having already missed the recovery.

Figure 2.3 illustrates broader performance differences across a longer time frame and more asset classes.[6] Unfortunately, it's hard to find anything that did worse than the average investor. If taxes had been included, the average investor would not have kept up with inflation.

**Figure 2.3**  20-Year Annualized Asset Class Returns (1991–2010)

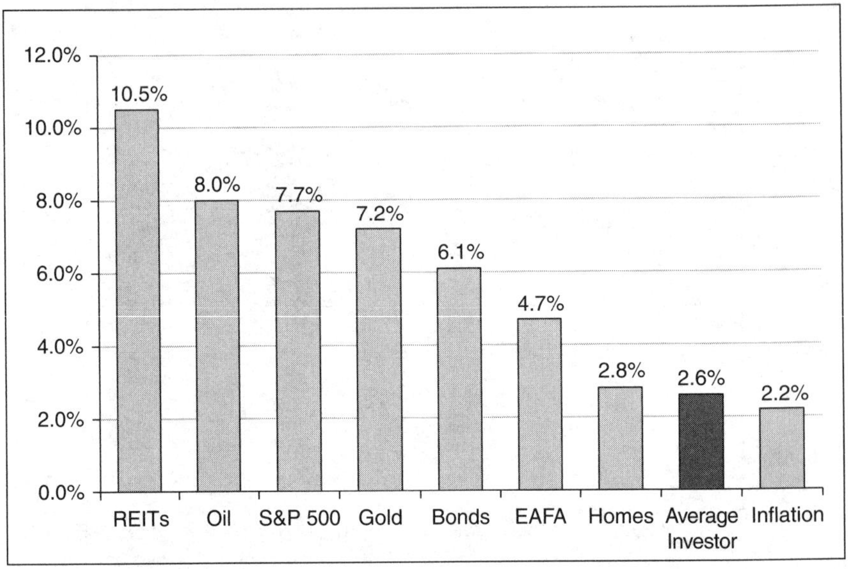

*Sources:* Indexes used are as follows: REITs: NAREIT equity REIT Index, EAFA: MSCI EAFA, Oil: WTI Index, Bonds: Barclays Capital U.S. Aggregate Index, Homes: median sale price of existing family home, Gold: USD troy ounce, Inflation: CPI.  Average asset allocation investor return is based on an analysis by Dalbar Inc., which utilizes the net aggregate mutual fund sales, redemptions, exchanges each month as a measure of investor behavior. Returns are annualized (and total return where applicable) and represent the 20-year period ending 12/31/10 to match Dalbar's study.

The terrible performance of the average investor is hard to overstate. No matter what measurement or performance criterion is used, individual investors struggle terribly.

The vast majority of mutual funds are invested in either stocks or bonds, so a quick assessment of the severity of the underperformance can be gained easily from looking at stocks or bonds. Both of these categories more than doubled the annualized performance of the average investor, and stock performance, as represented by the S&P 500, was almost triple. These numbers also underreport the difference. A very large percentage of stocks outperform the S&P 500 because most stocks are smaller than the stocks in the S&P 500. As a whole, small stocks have historically outperformed larger stocks. A measure of the broad-based market would show an even greater performance differential.

## Primary Causes

While there are different causes for investor underperformance, and some studies are quite comprehensive in listing various problems, in my experience, a few bad habits seem to cause the majority of the performance troubles. First, many investors attempt to time the market. Financial professionals are familiar with this tendency and even make the common assumption, which is usually correct, that the best time to invest is when individuals start heading for the exits. Conversely, when individual investors are all piling in, the market is probably nearing a high.

Mutual fund inflows and outflows illustrate this point far too well. Inflows into equity mutual funds reached record highs in late 1999 and early 2000, just before the dot-com crash that saw the S&P 500 fall nearly 40 percent. Conversely, mutual fund outflows hit record levels in October 2008, shortly before the U.S. stock market started its strongest bull market run in history.[7]

Second, even when individuals don't leave the market altogether, their actions still tend to be detrimental. Individual investors frequently sell their current holdings to buy funds that have performed better in the recent past than the funds they currently hold. They may be fleeing a fund that has struggled, or they may be pursuing something that has done particularly well recently. If you've ever switched your money out of a fund and reinvested it in a similar fund because the second fund was doing better, you're guilty. If this isn't you, congratulate yourself on avoiding a common, expensive pitfall of the mutual fund investor.

A paper titled "Dumb Money" by professors from the University of Chicago and Yale University highlights the propensity of individuals to mismanage their money. Very simply, the study found that the average investor moves their money from their current mutual funds into different funds with lower future returns, resulting in reducing their returns by between 4.3 percent and 10 percent per year, depending upon the time frame analyzed.[8] Those are big numbers.

Unfortunately, as we will cover in the next chapter, hot-performing funds tend to be hot for only a short time, then they underperform the market after their brief success. After switching to the once-hot fund, investors repeat the cycle when the new fund's performance cools. Buying high and selling low always hurts.

In addition, many investors incur more sales fees when they move from one fund into another, further increasing the already high fees of mutual funds.

To put it another way, most mutual fund investors are their own worst enemy. So, while the average mutual fund lags far behind most of the major indexes, investors exacerbate this problem by further sabotaging their investment performance.

Many mutual fund investors remind me of a man I saw driving on a highway in 1990 at a border crossing in Europe. Before Europe removed its passport and vehicle inspections at border crossings, traffic delays and long lines were common. At the border to enter Austria from Germany, my wife and I found ourselves in a two-hour-long traffic backup.

Obviously, sitting in a long line of cars on a hot day pleased no one, but there was one particularly impatient driver who stood out from the rest. As traffic inched forward, he kept changing lanes, attempting to find the lane with the faster traffic. Unfortunately, as soon as he switched lanes, traffic in his new lane slowed down. Often, the speed in his original lane then picked up, propelling cars behind him past his position.

Not surprisingly, he became frustrated with the slow speed of his new lane and switched back to the original lane—just as it slowed down. He became more and more frustrated, and he looked downright furious as he worked himself backwards relative to the other drivers. I can still remember the bulging veins on his red forehead.

He would done far better to relax and stay put in either lane, and he certainly would have endured less stress.

The driver's experience parallels the experience of many investors who switch into different mutual funds and even different investment vehicles that have recently enjoyed unusual success. DALBAR estimates that, on average, mutual fund investors now hold their funds for only 3.3 years as they routinely switch from one holding to another.[9]

Just as lanes speed up and slow down over time, mutual funds often follow a very similar pattern. Cambridge Associates, another financial research firm, reports that over the last 10 years, 98 percent of top-ranked fund managers performed poorly during at least one period lasting three years.[10] Underperformance for shorter periods is inevitable for any investor, including mutual fund managers.

While I have referred to mutual fund investors, the same principles and statistics regarding timing the market generally apply to equity investors who move into and out of the market via any other investment vehicle. Chasing specific strategies and investments that have enjoyed recent success tends to result in problems similar to those related to chasing hot mutual funds. If a strategy has recently enjoyed outstanding success, it may be less likely to do well in the immediate future.

For many individuals, a last major cause of poor performance is paying fees that are either too high or simply entirely inappropriate. In my experience, fees tend to be poorly understood and badly managed. Or investors take the opposite approach and seek to avoid all fees, regardless of the value they provide.

To be clear, I'm not saying that you should avoid paying fees. There are costs associated with all types of investing, and if you invest, you will pay fees. There is simply no way around this. Even the most sophisticated investors on the planet pay fees.

Since many of the fees are paid for services that can be very valuable, the goal is to pay the right fees for the right service. There is no magic number or ideal arrangement that clearly outlines acceptable costs for specific services. In addition, investors differ from one another, making no single arrangement ideal for everyone. Rather, the target for any investor should be avoiding many of the most egregious fees that often provide little or no value, while still enjoying services that are understood and valued.

This is probably simpler than it sounds because fees exist in so many areas and can creep in unnoticed so easily. Some fees can be worth far more than investors realize, whereas many others remain only because investors don't understand how little value particular services provide. Fortunately, once you raise your awareness of fees, making wise choices usually becomes fairly straightforward. It's like deciding whether to take a plane, a car, or a bike across country or across town. The choice will often be obvious, but many investors fail to even consider their options or understand the implications of different choices.

The topic of fees will come up in many sections of this book because of their constant presence. The greater point here is realizing that this is an issue that needs managing. Avoiding unnecessary fees offers real benefits, as does adding useful services.

## What Drives Investors

It would seem that investors should have learned from their past mistakes and adjusted their behavior. Yet in spite of all our experience and our knowledge about the subject, the pattern repeats in good and bad markets. Decades ago, financial professionals tended to assume that individuals just needed to show more discipline or act more rationally. While this would help, decades of similar behavior throughout many diverse economic and market conditions, in spite of vastly greater availability of information and experience, suggest a more intransigent problem.

Psychologists, researchers, and personal experience suggest a few common human characteristics that drive individual behavior and are very difficult to change. No list can cover everything, as people are very complicated, but I believe most major causes can be identified fairly easily.

No investor wants to inflict harm on him or herself. Moreover, most people are quite intelligent. While all of us are guilty of making bad decisions occasionally, overall, we tend to learn and make pretty good choices in most areas of our lives. Yet for some reason, we can't seem to get investing consistently right, or, often, even close to right. Why?

A major cause appears to be our natural defense mechanisms. In nature, if everyone else is running from a perceived danger, it's usually wise to join in and determine the exact peril later—after we've gotten to safety. When we're investing, this behavior is often disastrous. When most people are running for safety, the wisest action is very often to run into the fire rather than fleeing.

Psychologists also believe that fear is a much stronger motivator than nearly anything else. This makes taking the most rational action much more difficult when we are faced with the fear of losing money. Our overwhelming desire to avoid loss can make sensible action, such as buying more of whatever people are selling at a discount, much more difficult.

If we could somehow apply the discipline we have when we buy consumable items to buying stocks, our investment behavior would probably be much more rational. When people are shopping for groceries, almost all of them believe that high prices are bad and low prices are good. If you can usually buy a dozen eggs for $2.99, and you saw a sign at the store that read, "Manager's Special: One Dozen Eggs for only $22.99!!" would you buy them? Of course not. So what would happen to the eggs? They would sit there. Once the manager realized the error, the price would be changed. A new price might be $0.99 a dozen. The eggs would now be a bargain, and they would fly off the shelf.

With stocks and any asset we buy as an investment, it can be hard to think that way. When the price of an investment is high, investors usually want more of it. When the price is low, the current holders have losses, and potential investors often avoid it, partly because it may keep going down. With an investment, we extrapolate today's value into the future and assume, usually incorrectly, that the price will continue moving up or down.

The difference seems to lie in a very simple but very important distinction between an investment and anything that we consume. When we make an investment, we are planning to consume or use the asset sometime in the unknown future. Therefore, the possibility of its declining indefinitely is scary. It represents a potential loss of future security, and it's entirely rational to avoid loss of a future benefit.

Groceries are different. We'll eat them almost immediately, so valuing them is much easier, since their worth is closely tied to an experience we can relate to today.

For most individual investors, investing in a mediocre or poor market doesn't feel good. We all like to be part of the winning team. When we buy stock in a down market, it feels like we're buying a loser and possibly giving our money away. If the market keeps going down, we feel especially foolish.

Obviously, most people feel better investing in a market that's trending upward or even at record highs. Buying winners is so much more fun, and it seems so rational. If the market has been going up, it should keep going up. And as long as stock prices continue increasing, we feel good. Seemingly, all our survival training has wired us to feel better buying high and selling low.

Our preprogrammed risk/reward measurement system intro-duces an undesirable dynamic. Most market-based investments that provide values on a daily basis overpunish short-term failure and overreward short-term success. We are designed to make short-term survival trade-offs, and we have outstanding abilities to make fast and nuanced decisions on complex issues.

But investing is different. For most people, investing needs to have a long-term focus. We don't tend to make these decisions as easily, especially if we're punished severely in the short term for actions that we're not sure will work well in the long term.

In addition, with most assets, we don't have all the relevant data in front of us. The data can be too great and too complex, or simply incomplete. They're rarely clear. These challenges can make sensible action very difficult.

Moreover, investing can also require incredible discipline, possibly more than many of us possess—or at least can comfortably exercise. Investors know that they shouldn't panic, and that asset values should come back, but what if this time is different? It's too easy to join with everyone else and seek safety, rather than braving uncertainty and enduring losses in the short term. Given these factors, it's not surprising that so many investors fall short on a regular basis.

Of course, individuals make rational long-term decisions all the time. However, the dynamics are often very different. If you made the choice to go to college, you had a very high level of confidence that your effort would be well rewarded in the future. You knew the general time frame involved and the trade-offs of cost versus potential benefit. In the short term, you had to put in some effort, but the overall experience was probably fairly enjoyable and even rewarding, and an excellent future payoff was highly probable.

In contrast, investing can present much less rewarding circumstances. You may add an investment that immediately declines in value, and the future is almost always ill defined. Will your investment grow? If so, when and by how much? In the meantime, uncertainty and volatility can make the best decisions appear imprudent.

I mention all this to make a basic point. Taking the right action, even if you know exactly what it is, will often be difficult, particularly when you are using the standard investment approach of including only stocks and bonds. The dynamics of the model are very difficult to manage because they blatantly clash with most of our programmed decision criteria.

Moreover, the challenge is unlikely to become easier. Technology continues to increase the speed of money flows. More trading decisions are driven and completed by computers. Greater access to information and faster implementation of investment decisions on multiple levels by a wide variety of investors moves markets more quickly. Increasing global volatility is likely to contribute to the problem rather than making the decisions easier.

In addition, individual investors have more information, but it's rarely the right information. Most data are immediate and near-term in focus and completely lack a long-term perspective or inclusion of an investment's inherent complexity.

As we move forward and seek an approach that will be successful, addressing investors' overwhelming tendency to take the wrong action at the wrong time will be an important part of developing a successful strategy. A good strategy has the potential to meet an investor's financial goals, but, not surprisingly, it works only if it's followed. If it's too hard to implement or too easy to abandon, the terrible numbers already mentioned become too common.

Next, we're going to go through challenges of various traditional strategies and investment vehicles that investors use. As we go through these issues, it will become clearer why so many investors fall short of their objectives. It will also help us move closer to developing an approach to finances that can work well over longer and shorter time frames, and that is likely to remain in place during the inevitable uncertainty and volatility.

## 3

# Limitations of Traditional Approaches

MANY INVESTORS HAVE STRUGGLED TO ACHIEVE THE INVESTMENT success they assumed was within their reach when they made their plans. While the previous chapter addressed some of the reasons that people's investments fall short of their potential, part of the problem results from the overall investment approach, not just investor management.

The traditional investment approach that uses only domestic stocks and bonds has struggled horribly in the first decade plus of the new millennium. I believe this model is likely to continue to present its followers with many challenges over the next few years and even decades. Parts of the strategy can work well, but the overall approach has severe limitations that often make success very difficult.

Beyond strategy limitations, there are issues with some of today's most common investments, mutual funds, that can expose investors to significant, and often unrecognized, pitfalls. These shortcomings can add greatly to the problems of poor strategy and destructive investor behavior.

Finally, various poor investment practices often pass for respectable investment strategies. Some of these approaches are quite common, or are seen by investors as potential answers to the problems presented by other investment approaches. They can tempt investors, but they usually cause more harm than good, and we might as well eliminate them from consideration. Looking at a few of these approaches will highlight some common problems and should help you avoid poor choices. Hopefully, none of your practices will be in here, but if they are, this section could save you future problems—and pain.

## Traditional Investment Approach

Many investors, especially those who are near or in retirement, follow some version of a stock and bond approach with an approximate allocation of 60 percent to stocks and 40 percent to bonds. Although allocations may differ, with a somewhat lower or higher allocation to stocks, a portfolio composed of around 60 percent stocks and 40 percent bonds remains incredibly common.

This allocation became particularly popular because academic research indicated that it offered a very attractive balance of risk versus reward. The foundation for the academic research was Harry Markowitz's 1952 article, "Portfolio Selection," and subsequent work that eventually won him a Nobel Prize in 1990.[1]

Markowitz's work focused on maximizing the expected return for a specific level of risk or minimizing risk for a given level of return, a concept called modern portfolio theory (MPT). The means used to adjust risk and return were stocks and bonds. At the time, the paper was groundbreaking, even though Markowitz himself called his concept "portfolio theory" because, he said, there was nothing modern about it. The concept established an easily understood and implemented framework for adjusting the estimated risk and return of a portfolio.

While MPT has been criticized in recent years for various reasons, including limitations in scope and oversimplification, its impact on the investment community is undeniable because its framework became so pervasive. Today's assumption that adding stocks and decreasing bonds in a portfolio increases risk is largely derived from his research.

While Markowitz's work introduced various ideas, some of the most impactful and long-lasting have been assumptions concerning the use of changes in the relative percentages of stocks and bonds to alter the expected returns and volatility of a portfolio. Yet, the framework provides only a model of likely or possible performance, rather than precise prescriptions for the ideal portfolio. And, the model changes with the use of data from different time frames. The easily understood framework has helped investors make decisions regarding their investments, but the model's inherent ambiguity doesn't offer exact choices.

Over many years and many different time frames, the financial services industry has largely agreed that a portfolio with approximately 60 percent stocks and 40 percent bonds was at or near the inflection point at which increasing the allocation to stocks increased risk faster than return. At stock allocations lower than 60 percent, the risk increased more slowly than the reward, but not by much. As stock allocations decline to closer to 40 percent, expected portfolio return is usually assumed to fall faster than risk, but again, not by too much. Once stocks decline to below a 40 percent allocation, however, expected return is generally assumed to fall significantly faster than the corresponding risk.

As a result, portfolios with around 40 to 60 percent stocks and 60 to 40 percent bonds became the standard model, because of the expectation that they offered the most attractive balance of expected return for a given level of risk. Since the 60 percent stock allocation produces a level of volatility that many have seen as acceptable for people in or near retirement, and since increasing stock allocations up to this point was assumed to increase expected return as fast as risk, this portfolio has largely become the standard option, seen to offer the best balance of expected return versus potential risk.

This allocation made tremendous sense in the years after 1952, when the original study was done, and when investors had very few investment options outside of stocks and bonds.

Many resources in the financial services industry were devoted to helping investors create, implement, and manage strategies based on the principles originally espoused by modern portfolio theory. And the popularity of the model grew for many years, as strategies based on these principles provided reasonable returns and seemingly confirmed the theory's merit.

The theory provided the investment community and investors with a straightforward framework and a common language that fostered easier and clearer communication on a complex topic that was new to most investors. The model's elegance also quickly explained specific risk levels and means to easily adjust expected portfolio volatility up or down.

Moreover, decades ago, markets were much less volatile, partly because buying and selling was much more difficult. If you are old enough, you probably remember limitations that restricted changes to your retirement plan allocations to one time per quarter via a special written request form. Investors suffered through ups and downs more easily, partly because they had no choice. They often couldn't change their investment allocations without significant cost or hassle.

While many criticisms of the model are common today, the one that is probably most accurate and relevant for individual investors is the charge that the model fails to include assets other than domestic stocks and bonds, and thereby provides much more limited opportunities for returns and far greater exposure to volatility.

In 1952, using only these assets made sense largely because they were essentially the only tradable investments available. Today's world is very different. Limiting yourself to these two asset classes no longer seems sensible, and performance since the turn of the century provides ample illustration of the model's shortcomings.

A few basic performance numbers provide tremendous insight. From the turn of the century through 2011, the annualized 12-year return for a 60 percent stock and 40 percent bond portfolio falls short of 3 percent per year, reaching only a 2.92 percent annualized return.

While this return is obviously quite anemic, it's probably substantially better than what the average investor earned over the same period. The indexes are not available for direct investment, and their returns reflect no fees that an investor would incur. Furthermore, the return numbers exclude all the performance deficiencies mentioned earlier that so many average investors incur.

If we combine the average underperformance of individual stock and bond investors that we covered earlier with these data, the numbers drop dramatically. Figure 2.1 showed that the average investor trailed the S&P 500 by 4.3 percent per year and trailed the Barclays Aggregate Bond Index by 5.6 percent over the 20 years ending in 2011. If we apply these numbers to the actual return percentages, the 60 percent stock and 40 percent bond portfolio lost 1.9 percent per year, or more than 20 percent of its value, over the 12-year period.

Obviously, some investors would have done markedly better, but I also know from professional experience that many investors, unfortunately, did far worse.

However, most larger investors succeeded over the same time period. For example, the endowments of Yale, Harvard, and Stanford earned a combined average return of 10.88 percent per year from the beginning of 2000 through 2011.[2] Unlike the hypothetical index returns cited earlier, these numbers are realized return numbers, net of all fees and expenses. One dollar invested in these endowments would have grown to $3.45, while our hypothetical average individual would have seen his dollar shrink to only $0.79 when the Dalbar 20-year average investor underperformance is included. Figure 3.1 displays the tremendous differences in performance among these potential investors.

While not all the differences in performance can be attributed to the endowments' abandonment of a tired 60/40 portfolio approach, their adoption of much more advanced strategies including far more types of investments is the major contributing factor to their superior performance.

**Figure 3.1** Growth of $1 with Different Strategies (2000–2011)

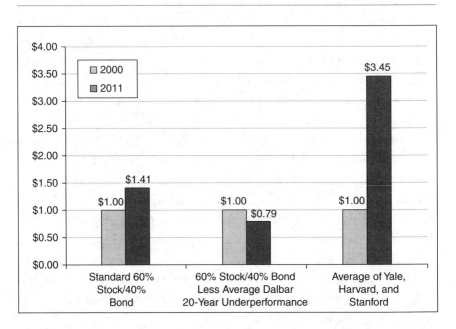

## Limitations of Mutual Funds

Beyond portfolio structure, which determines the general types of assets in a portfolio, such as stocks and bonds, the means of securing exposure to specific types of investments can also significantly affect investors' performance.

Nearly all investors in the United States are familiar with mutual funds, largely because they own or have owned them. They've been the financial services industry's answer to seemingly every question for decades. If you have a 401(k) retirement plan, mutual funds are probably the only type of investment you can hold in the account.

### Structure of Mutual Funds

Let's start by making sure we understand what these animals are. A mutual fund pools funds from various investors into one common, or "mutual," fund. A money manager invests the aggregated funds by purchasing securities on behalf of the mutual fund. The securities that the fund has purchased, along with any cash or any other investments of the fund, are considered the fund's holdings or assets. Mutual fund shareholders own shares in the mutual fund based on their proportional investment in the total pool of funds.

The value of a mutual fund is the combined value of all the holdings or assets of the fund less all of its liabilities. The fund's net asset value is divided into smaller pieces, referred to as shares, so that investors can easily buy and sell small parts of the fund. The value of these shares is referred to as net asset value per share, or NAV. In general, the net asset value per share is the price an investor receives when selling a share back to the fund. All this structure is set up so that a mutual fund can pool investments from different people, buy securities, and sell representative ownership in the securities it has purchased.

## A Great Concept

Mutual funds are a great concept, and they were one of the fastest-growing means of investing until the market turmoil starting in 2000. They allowed small investors into the Wall Street game when it was very difficult for the average person to invest in the stock market. When commissions ran hundreds or thousands of dollars per trade, mutual funds provided a great way to invest in the market easily, since there was often no per trade cost to purchase a mutual fund.

In addition, for many, if not most, investors, mutual funds provided greater diversification than they could achieve on their own. Because the fund manager had a much larger pool of money to invest than the individual investor, she had ample funds available to buy a representative sample of companies. Through investment in the fund, investors could easily own small amounts of numerous companies at low cost.

The concept's wide acceptance resulted in explosive growth. By the end of 2011, 44 percent of U.S. households owned mutual funds, compared with only 5.7 percent in 1980,[3] and U.S. investment companies managed $13.0 trillion in net assets,[4] which is nearly one-quarter of all U.S. household assets. Not surprisingly, these numbers grew rapidly during the boom years of the 1980s and 1990s. From 2000 to the end of 2011, however, mutual funds' share of U.S. household net worth has edged up only a percentage point or two,[5] and the number of fund companies has declined by almost 10 percent.[6] While their popularity isn't rising as fast as it once was, they still retain a dominant position within the investment world.

Mutual funds however, were conceived and developed when the market looked very different from the way it looks today. Technology advances and the creation of competing products have created a completely different investment landscape from the one that existed during mutual funds' decades of rapid growth. Today, many of their original advantages no longer offer investors value, and new developments may make other investment vehicles a better choice.

Better understanding of mutual funds' advantages and drawbacks can help greatly in understanding when and how they can best be employed by various investors. Like most investments, they are not absolutely bad or always good. Rather, they tend to be frequently misused.

## Times Have Changed

As we all know, technology has greatly changed our world and continues to do so at an accelerating pace. Technological advances have changed nearly every area of the financial services industry and have helped individuals gain much easier and cheaper access to the stock market. In many cases, the positive changes have eliminated the original advantages of mutual funds while highlighting many of their deficiencies.

When trading fees were sky high and stockbrokers were the only people with access to good information, successful investing was difficult for the small investor. Even if an investor made great choices, fees could eat up profits and substantially drag down returns.

Not only have the difficulty and expense of trading stocks decreased, but costs have plummeted to almost negligible amounts.

It's now impossible to avoid commercials for low-cost trades if you watch nearly any sporting event. Years ago, buying and selling shares was tremendously laborious. Now, it's highly efficient and inexpensive.

And, of course, many, many other activities have been automated. When you buy a stock, a brokerage house records that you own the stock, but the certificate never moves or even changes ownership. In fact, technically you don't even own the stock; you just have a claim to it. The certificates are stored in the basement of a building near Wall Street and never move. The brokerage company holds them for you in its name. This is quite a change from the practice years ago that required the delivery of a physical certificate to the shareholder after every transaction.

With all this drastic change in the investment world, mutual funds are no longer the best option for many, if not most, individual investors. Investors are increasingly recognizing this and voting with their dollars. Mutual funds' deficiencies generally fall into several distinct categories.

- The vast majority of funds underperform the general market. Mutual funds have large overheads and expenses that are passed on to the investors, contributing to underperformance.
- Taxes incurred by mutual funds as a result of trading can further reduce actual investor returns.
- Investor returns are usually much lower than current numbers indicate because of "survivorship bias" and "creation bias," discussed later in this chapter. In effect, only the winning mutual funds are measured against the market.

## Mutual Fund Performance

When mutual funds were first introduced, they opened up new opportunities for the average investor. Because these funds often provided a superior means to invest in the stock market, most investors were much less concerned that their funds weren't the best performers. In addition, it was really hard to tell how well any particular fund was doing. It wasn't as if you owned IBM or GE. Instead, you owned XYZ Premier Growth Fund or ABC Large Cap Value Fund. If the market went up and your fund did too, you were happy. If the market went down and so did your fund, you were consoled by the fact that everyone else was also losing money. Since most funds tracked the general market fairly closely, as long as they trended in the same general direction as the market, most investors were satisfied.

As the industry matured, however, more information became available, and ratings agencies sprang up. Morningstar, a company that rates mutual fund performance by assigning stars to mutual funds, was founded in 1984. The firm rose to prominence because it offered consolidated information and measurement of many mutual fund performance characteristics. Its ratings are also easily understood. A five-star rating means that the fund's relative performance has been great, while a one-star rating probably prompts the mutual fund company to begin looking for a new manager or planning the fund's dissolution.

Interestingly, much of the best research on mutual fund performance originated several years, if not decades, ago. When mutual fund inflows were rapidly swelling the category's size, academics and other industry specialists seemed to be making more of an effort to educate individuals on the many limitations of the product, and there was more opportunity to perform original research. Since many of the deficiencies are well documented today, the motivation to focus on mutual funds' problems appears to have declined. The struggle of equity markets over the last decade has probably contributed to less attention being paid to particular mutual funds as well.

Regardless, their underperformance remains quite notable. According to *Fortune* magazine, the average equity fund trailed the S&P 500 stock index by about 3 percent from 1982 through 2002.[7] This number probably understates the problem because the average equity fund doesn't emulate the S&P 500, but adopts some other strategy or focuses on a particular sector with higher expected performance. The S&P 500 represents approximately the largest 500 companies in the United States. Over time, it's been well documented that smaller-company stocks outperform larger-company stocks, albeit with higher volatility. Since the average equity fund referred to by *Fortune* will include many mutual funds with higher performance expectations, comparing all equity funds to the lower-performing S&P 500 isn't accurate.

A *Wall Street Journal* article from August 2005 refers to more detailed research by Rob Arnott, a well-respected researcher of equity markets, stock indexes, and mutual funds. Data referred to in the article illustrate that the 10-year after-tax returns of mutual funds trail the returns you would have earned in an index fund (an index fund simply mimics a specific equity index like the S&P 500, but still has some costs) by 4.5 percent per year.[8] He cites various reasons for the performance gap, including fees, taxes, and survivorship bias, which will be addressed shortly.

It might be tempting to ignore these data if you have access to various ratings services, such as the already mentioned Morningstar. It seems pretty obvious that a prudent step to eliminate the performance problem could be to select only higher-rated funds. And, since an incredible 75 percent of one-star-rated funds holding both stocks and bonds disappeared within five years, this strategy could seem well advised.[9]

Unfortunately, a fund's previous year's outperformance tends to be an indicator that the fund will underperform in the future. A recently completed study bears this out. Stock and bond funds that were given the number one performance ranking of five stars each year were analyzed to see their results for the following three-, five-, and ten-year periods. The results are discouraging. A full 80 percent of the top-rated funds performed worse than the average similar fund over the different time periods. In fact, some of the top-rated funds ended up at or near the bottom of future ranking charts.[10] Many other similar studies show similar results.

Unfortunately, investments in mutual funds often seem doomed from the start, since most funds underperform the market so severely in any given year. And, if you're more diligent and research funds to identify better-performing possibilities, you may do no better because these funds as a group have historically underperformed in subsequent years relative to similar funds that are already underperforming the market.

So, if this is true, why do people continue to choose a losing proposition? I believe the reasons range from lack of knowledge to resignation that better options are not available.

Many people have no idea of their fund's performance relative to either its peers or the general market. The confusion over its relative and absolute performance often masks the fact that the fund is simply performing poorly. If the fund is underperforming the market, people may think it's because a particular sector isn't doing well. Or if a fund is keeping up with the market, it still may be a laggard in its industry class, and the investor was fortunate to land in a hot industry. Either way, there are many reasons that investors may not understand how well their fund is doing.

In my experience, many investors also still believe that with enough research and a little luck, they can pick the elusive and rare exceptional outperforming fund. This belief is fueled by the fact that there have been a few, and I mean a very few, notable exceptions to the trend of mediocrity that gives investors hope that their fund will be different.

One of the most famous and successful fund managers of all time is Peter Lynch. He became famous through his 13 successful years of managing a large and famous mutual fund at Fidelity. Over his tenure, he managed to return an astounding average annual rate of 29.2 percent.[11]

Unfortunately, Peter Lynch retired because his job was overwhelming him, and there hasn't been anybody else who has really even approached his record. Many people, however, keep investing in mutual funds hoping to find the next big hit. We all want to believe that somewhere out there is the mutual fund version of a lottery ticket. Instead, with great regularity, investors earn mediocre returns that trail the market.

Why is this? How can professional money managers trail the market? Let's look at Peter Lynch again. As the leading fund manager, one would think that he would be a proponent of mutual funds. He's seen them work, and his association with a mutual fund made him famous. His comments in one of his books are enlightening. After talking about three individuals who did exceedingly well in the markets, but are not fund managers themselves, Mr. Lynch says:

> These notable exceptions are entirely outnumbered by the run-of-the-mill fund managers, dull fund managers, comatose fund managers, sycophantic fund managers, timid fund managers, plus other assorted camp followers, fuddyduddies, and copycats hemmed in by the rules.[12]

Those are strong words from someone who knows this business very well. And the evidence supports his accusation. Mutual funds consistently underperform the market. Let's look into a few reasons why.

## Fees

In addition to mediocre fund managers, the most significant reason that mutual funds perform so poorly is related to their internal costs. Since the net asset value of a fund is equal to the value of all the fund's assets less all its liabilities, every dollar of expenses that the fund incurs drives up its liabilities and therefore decreases its share price.

The relationship to performance should be relatively obvious here. Simply put, when a fund spends money, it's your money that's being spent. The higher the costs of any fund, the better the performance required to cover those costs. And, as the previous discussion indicated, most fund managers are not gifted with tremendous insight and creativity, but rather are members of a rather dull, directionless herd. Given this fact, most investors can increase their funds' performance simply by choosing low-cost funds. With this in mind, let's cover the major expenses.

### Sales Load

The most obvious expense to most people is the sales load. For class A shares, which pay a broker an up-front commission, sales loads will range up to and over 5 percent. Many, if not most, investors no longer pay up-front sales fees because they avoid class A shares. This doesn't mean, however, that they pay no sales fees. Many loaded funds invest 100 percent of your money up front and simply pay a sales commission to brokers through a deferred sales load over a period of time rather than up front.

As fee-based accounts have grown in popularity, sales charges have become less common, eliminating an obvious investment cost. Yet, even though sales fees often receive a great deal of investor scrutiny, these fees are rarely the largest fee associated with mutual funds.

### 12b-1 Fees

This strangely named fee is a little-known but often expensive fee that can cost far more than a sales load over time. The fee was originally imposed to enable smaller fund companies to charge additional marketing and distribution fees while growing the fund. In theory, once the funds grew larger, economies of scale would kick in, and the fees would decrease. This kind of sounds like the argument put forth to justify "temporary" taxes. As you can imagine, once the fees are in, they're difficult to eliminate.

### Expense Ratio

All funds have an expense ratio. The only difference among funds is the size of the ratio. The expense ratio is the percentage of fund assets used on an annual basis to pay for expenses, such as registration costs, legal fees, prospectus costs, fund manager salaries, marketing costs, office space, and so on. Largely because of Morningstar's reporting services, most investors understand expense ratios and realize that higher expenses often hinder performance.

Most expense ratios remain fairly "reasonable," and after rising through 1999, they have dropped a bit over last decade or so. As you would expect, they affect fund performance. Expense ratios usually range between 1 and 2 percent and rarely climb much above 2.5 percent, especially for funds offered by the larger and better-known fund companies, although I've seen them be as high as 10 percent per year. The average expense ratio in 2011 was 1.43 percent.[13] However, while expense fees will eat up more of your return over time than any sales load will, they are often not the greatest expense that your fund will absorb. That distinction is left to a cost that few people, including investment professionals, are aware of.

*Turnover Costs*

Turnover costs tend to be poorly understood, even by financial professionals, because they are nearly impossible to document, are not part of the information required in a mutual fund prospectus, and don't show up in a Morningstar report. Turnover costs are incurred by a mutual fund when it trades a stock. Because most funds are large and trade large volumes of stock, their trading costs per share are much lower than most individuals could get on their own. Many mutual funds, however, deliberately overpay for trading as a means of compensating the firms that distribute their products.

Depending on which study and time frame is used, turnover costs tend to hover around 0.80 percent,[14] although certain studies post much higher numbers.

John Bogle, the founder and ex-chairman of Vanguard funds, talks about this in his book. He says, "A 1993 study in the *Financial Analysts Journal* suggested the cost of an average transaction was equivalent to 6/10's of 1 percent. Many other studies suggest substantially higher transaction costs, ranging from 1.0 to 2.0 percent."[15] I'll be conservative and use the lower cost estimates.

Given that it's common for turnover rates to exceed 100 percent, this fee can become quite substantial for many funds. For example, if the turnover in a fund is 100 percent, you would pay 0.6 percent to sell the stocks it holds once, and then another 0.6 percent to replace them, for a total of 1.2 percent.

A 2009 study of mutual funds in retirement accounts identified the average expense ratio at 1.46 percent, which is very close to the 1.43 percent estimated for equity mutual funds in general. But then an additional 1.63 percent in turnover costs was also calculated, adding up to a total of 3.09 percent annual costs for equity funds.[16] These fees were for retirement account assets, which generally contain pretty good funds because of the initial and ongoing scrutiny of the funds.

### Market Impact Costs

Mutual funds, particularly large ones, suffer from another cost. When they buy stocks, they often move the market and increase their average share purchase price.

If you buy a stock, chances are that you'll purchase all your shares at the same price. If you place a market order (a regular, plain vanilla buy order) and the market has the shares priced at $50, you'll get all your shares for the price of $50.

When a mutual fund with billions of dollars in assets invests millions or hundreds of millions of dollars in one company, it can dramatically alter the share price. The mutual fund may start buying shares at $50, but its demand for shares can outstrip the supply available at $50, in which case it must pay a greater amount to entice more sellers into the market. Prices can easily rise well above the original $50 per share price. This cost adds up, but it is often ignored because no one individual or institution is paid a fee, and it is often difficult to measure.

### Survivorship Bias

The performance numbers and fees that have been listed so far are further complicated by a couple of other factors. The numbers reported generally represent only currently active mutual funds, not all the mutual funds that generated returns during previous years. Total performance numbers drop again when the returns of all funds are tallied, including those of funds that were shut down, combined, or eliminated.

As you would hope, mutual fund companies are usually run by very bright people. As expected, these individuals are interested in growing their fund company, and they are well aware that current and potential investors focus on return numbers. Given this simple fact, it's obvious that a company can attract more investors if its funds perform well. Better returns tend to generate more capital inflows.

The numbers and statistics already covered were all calculated on existing mutual funds. By calculating mutual fund returns based on the funds that are currently in existence, however, we have, by definition, calculated only the returns of the winners.

The relative performance of funds determines their ratings, and the ratings affect a company's ability to attract new money into the fund. As already mentioned, 75 percent of funds with a one-star Morningstar rating disappear within five years. The natural result is that performance numbers for mutual funds include only the returns of the best mutual funds, since poorer funds disappear over time. When poor-performing funds are swept away, investors in the losing funds become investors in a new fund.

This practice introduces survivorship bias into returns, a constant upward revision of the returns earned by the average mutual fund. The average investor rarely considers survivorship bias, but the mutual fund industry, and particularly its marketing departments, is very aware of this phenomenon and uses it to the firm's advantage constantly. Again, much of the research is a bit dated, but the trends haven't changed much.

Approximately 3 percent of mutual funds were eliminated every year through the 1970s and 1980s.[17] A comprehensive study of mutual funds covering the period from 1962 to 1993 found that a full one-third of all the mutual funds being studied had simply disappeared.[18] As we move forward, we see that in 1996, 242 (5 percent) of the 4,555 stock funds tracked by Lipper Analytical Services were merged into other funds or liquidated. In 1998, 637 stock and bond funds were merged or liquidated out of existence.[19] In 2000, 451 funds were closed (223) or merged (222).[20] In 2010, the rate of fund mergers and liquidations remained about the same at 494 before dropping slightly in 2011 to 486.[21] The trend continues, with many statistics demonstrating remarkably consistent ongoing merging and elimination of poor-performing funds. Obviously, when funds are closed or merged, the number of losing funds decreases. The fund companies use this technique to raise their average, and the practice has an impact.

In 1986, the existing 586 stock funds yielded a return of 13.4 percent. If we fast-forward 10 years to 1996, this number had magically become 14.7 percent. Mutual fund performance increased 1.3 percent because 24 percent of the funds disappeared.[22] The funds that remained were the better-performing funds, thus raising the average stock fund performance. Various studies, including those just referred to, have found that mutual fund returns decrease on average around 10 percent if survivorship bias is included.

## Creation Bias

Similar to survivorship bias, which introduces an upward bias by closing funds, an upward bias can also be created by using clever tactics when starting a fund. If a mutual fund company aims to ensure a great launch of a new fund, there are various means it can use to manipulate the return numbers. One method is to start several funds simultaneously, then keep or promote only the fund with the best performance. Different funds invest in different stocks confined to a particular industry. The plan is that at least one of the funds will excel.

If one or more of the funds take off, the company chooses the best of the funds and closes the others. Once the fund has established a great performance record, managers can promote it using its great track record. Creation bias can also be a natural outcome of a competitive market. Successful funds tend to attract new investment, while less successful ones are closed, so the phenomenon tends to result naturally as investors target better-performing funds.

But creation bias can also result from more sinister actions. Some companies purposely start multiple funds with very aggressive strategies. Some will likely excel because they catch the right market trend or simply get lucky while others struggle, and are eventually closed. To build on the successful start, the fund that built a successful track record through a unique or risky strategy that is believed to be unsustainable changes its management style to a more conservative approach less likely to squander its past success. Investors may be investing in an entirely different fund with no resemblance to the fund that earned outstanding returns.

As the funds that didn't make the cut are closed, they're effectively eliminated from mutual fund performance. The losers are left out, and only the winners are included. Creation bias can significantly add to the overall performance of mutual funds, but unfortunately, new investors don't actually benefit from this higher return.

Creation bias can also result from more mundane events. Instead of a company's planning to manipulate a fund's return to artificially high levels, a small fund simply gets lucky and does extraordinarily well in a given year. Let's say the fund achieves a 50 percent return in one year. The fund's performance generates publicity, and the mutual fund company promotes its success. Investment dollars flood in, and the fund balloons to ten times its original size. The next year, the fund is less fortunate and generates a 10 percent loss, resulting in a positive 16 percent two-year annualized return. The fund still looks great and can promote its good numbers.

The vast majority of investors, however, in what has become a large fund are down 10 percent. The performance numbers give the appearance of excellent performance, but the reality for most investors is very different. The fund's official return numbers bear no resemblance to the return earned by 90 percent of the fund's investors.

Finally, another form of creation bias occurs even when a fund is introduced with good intentions and complete transparency. A fund that appeared to be set for success doesn't always meet expectations. If a new fund without name recognition and size fails to generate attractive returns, it's obviously not going to be attractive to new investors. We've already mentioned that the people running the mutual fund companies are very sensitive to this obvious fact. Rather than trying to rescue a flailing fund and sell a weak performer to investors in a competitive market, they merge the fund with an existing fund. The poor performer is quietly ushered off the stage, never to be heard from again. (This looks like survivorship bias, but it is normally categorized as creation bias because the funds are closed soon after their creation rather than after a multiyear history.)

When this happens, it further introduces creation bias into mutual fund numbers. The fund's poor performance ceases to be counted the day it's merged with another fund. The net effect is that mutual fund average return numbers are improved by a marketing decision that helps no investors. Many of these actions take place without malicious intent. They're simply good business for a mutual fund company. For the average investor, however, they contribute to misleading performance information.

## Taxes

Mutual funds also have another unattractive hidden cost that affects your return, but not theirs. This expense is taxes. The mutual fund's only concern is achieving the highest possible return. It makes the fund look better and promotes additional sales. The effect of taxes upon investors is usually ignored. But investors live in the real world, and taxes are a very real consideration.

In addition, taxes on mutual funds are not limited to long-term capital gains. Because mutual funds rarely consider the taxes that investors pay, trading to minimize taxes remains rare.

Taxes also tend to be highest at the worst times. Like any stock market investment, a mutual fund incurs most of its tax liability when it sells stocks that have increased in value. Unfortunately, sales of stocks by a mutual fund tend to be highest when the market is going down because larger numbers of investors are selling their shares back to the company. In a down market, disproportionately high taxes can make this investment even worse.

Some funds' performance can be affected drastically. The *Wall Street Journal* reported that fund returns could drop as much as 38 percent as a result of tax effects, while average decreases are probably closer to 20 to 25 percent.[23] The effect of taxes on mutual fund performance varies and some funds market themselves as tax sensitive, but most ignore tax effects.

## The Combination

If we add all the fees, biases, and taxes together, Rob Arnott's claim that mutual funds trail their respective index fund by 4.5 percent no longer sounds unreasonable. Unfortunately, investors who believe that avoiding mutual funds with sales loads solves their performance problems often experience something very different.

## Appalling Investment Approaches

While the issues already mentioned in this chapter have contributed to poor investor returns over many decades, a few particularly destructive investor habits and practices deserve mention. Hopefully, this section can either keep you from trying these self-destructive tactics or steer you away from them if they have ensnared you in the past.

### Market Timing

Market timing has a very simple goal. Rather than telling you which stock to invest in, market-timing systems seek to identify when you should hold any stocks and when you should avoid them completely. The goal of the system is to hold stocks when the market is going up and sell them before the market goes down.

This system ranks as one of the most seductive, and its commonsense rationale often fools people into making costly mistakes. The goal is so simple and the potential results seem so alluring. If it worked, it would be a brilliant strategy, and would provide a nearly perfect means for buying low and selling high. Unfortunately, something that's so easy to understand remains very difficult to execute successfully.

Investors who try to time the market seem to inevitably end up out of the market when they should be in, and in the market when they should be out. This usually happens when investors sell out near the bottom because the pain of losses becomes too great. Even when investors successfully manage to avoid additional losses by selling before the market declines further, very few investors capitalize on their decision by entering the market at a discounted level. Instead, they nearly always wait to get back into the market until the market has moved past their original sale level. The result is that they are paying even more than their liquidation price to get back into the market. Nearly all respected academics and seasoned investors assume that consistently timing the market is as difficult as catching lightning.

The recent financial meltdown provides a clear example of investors sabotaging their own returns. During 2008, when the stock market declined 37 percent, assets flowed out of mutual funds for the three of the four quarters of the year. This sounds intelligent. Fear-based selling continued, however, for seven of the eight quarters in 2009 and 2010, despite the market's fantastic returns of 26.5 percent and 15.1 percent in 2009 and 2010, respectively.[24] Investors were selling when they should have been buying.

In addition, the largest "intelligent" withdrawals in 2008 were in the fourth quarter, followed closely by the third quarter. These investors pulled their funds out near the bottom, and few of them reinvested their funds to enjoy the subsequent recovery.[25]

Market-timing strategies can resemble a piranha-infested river. It may look very tempting and promise a wonderful, cool, and refreshing experience. But once you've been seduced into the water, any short-term benefits painfully disappear. Lurking dangers quickly inflict damage and make the original decision appear very short-sighted. And, once you're back on solid ground, you'll realize that you left part of yourself, or your portfolio, behind as your price for better understanding.

## Stop-Loss Orders

This traditional trading strategy frequently deceives investors with its simplicity. Yet, just like market timing, stop-loss orders rarely boost returns because investors are in the wrong place at the wrong time.

Stop orders are orders to buy or sell a stock once a specific price, the stop price, is reached. Most investors are more familiar with stop-loss orders, or stop losses, that trigger when the price declines down to or past a specific price.

Some stock newsletters tout stop losses as a way to protect investors from portfolio losses when specific stocks decline or the market drops. By selling any stock that declines by more than a set amount or percentage, investors can shield themselves from losses greater than a predetermined amount. The concept sounds almost foolproof, and yet it's used only selectively by certain individuals in particular circumstances.

Traders seek to earn profits through active and frequent stock trading using specific systems. Trading signals are often derived from factors involving technical analysis, such as trend-line indicators, price momentum, moving averages, and the like. In these instances, traders are rarely concerned about the fundamentals of a company or long-term stock values, as these values have no bearing on their buy or sell decisions. Instead, trade decisions are based on very near term issues and price changes. In this environment, large losses must be avoided at all costs, and stop losses can be an invaluable tool.

By contrast, professional money managers rarely use stop losses because their buy and sell decisions are based on the intrinsic value of the company compared to its current market value. For this reason, a lower stock price, which is believed to be temporary, makes a stock more—not less—attractive. Selling shares after a slight decline will usually be counterproductive.

There can be instances in which a manager might employ a stop loss. The most common involves attempting to profit from a stock that is trading above the price the manager had targeted as the exit price and is continuing to climb higher. The idea is to move the stop loss up if the stock price keeps increasing. But more commonly, instead of ratcheting up the stop price, the stock price decreases and triggers the stop loss sale, resulting in a lower sales price than the manager would have gotten if the stock had simply been sold. Hence, this trading strategy is not very popular with money managers.

From the perspective of a money manager, there are a few additional issues surrounding stop losses. Exercising stop losses guarantees selling low and missing a possible upward correction because a holding has been automatically converted to cash. Market noise frequently moves positions 10 to 20 percent in short time frames and can easily trigger undesired sells. During times of volatile markets, stop losses can be extremely damaging, as investors often sell when the market goes down but sit in cash when it goes up.

One of the supposed benefits of a stop loss often proves to be very damaging in actual experience. Bad news can cause stock prices to gap down markedly rather than easing to or through a preset stop-loss price. In this situation, a stop loss may be exercised automatically at a very unfavorable price, often much lower than the stop-loss price. Frequently, prices then bounce back sharply, and investors would have been better served by holding onto the position or selling in a more considered manner.

Stop losses are often held up as a solution to protect investors against a falling market. This is simply illogical. If all stocks are going down, only the avoidance of all stocks can protect investors against losses, and the problems with market timing were already covered. If the entire market is trending downward, selling one stock after an 8 percent decline to buy another stock that will also go down 8 percent only results in excessive trading and more tax headaches. It also may magnify losses because the subsequent positions are probably those that were originally deemed less favorable. In a downward-trending market, you want to be holding your best position, not your third choice that you were forced into by an ill-considered trading strategy.

Unfortunately, one of the most common uses of stop losses remains selling stock trading or tip services to inexperienced investors. The concept sounds wonderful, and the allure strongly resembles the potential offered by market timing. Yet, like market timing, results in practice rarely reach the promised potential.

## Moving Forward

After running through so many different ways in which investors sabotage their investment returns, you may be wondering how you build a portfolio that will excel over time. That's the rest of the book!

Highlighting investors' underperformance along with its many causes helps illustrate the low odds of success if you follow the staid, traditional strategies developed decades ago. Following the herd in the investment world rarely proves to be the best route, as the odds are stacked heavily against you.

The popularity of these dated approaches results from entrenched systems, inflexible methodologies, and ease of implementation. Their frequent use rarely results from a high probability of success. The future investment climate also must be considered. Record low interest rates, expectations of rising inflation, and ongoing volatility all suggest that achieving success using these types of stale and dated strategies will be more difficult in the future rather than easier.

# 4

# The Traditional Model's Future

THE PREVIOUS CHAPTER EXPLORED THE MANY PROBLEMS INVESTORS have experienced over decades using the traditional stock and bond model. While it's obvious that I don't recommend the model for investors, not all parts of it should be abandoned. Both stocks and bonds have various attributes that can help many portfolios. Moreover, the future for both of them will probably differ from the recent past for numerous reasons.

## Stocks

Starting with stocks, the longer-term future for U.S. equities will probably see significantly higher returns than those achieved in the first 12 years of the new millennium. While there's never any guarantee that the market will perform as expected, several factors suggest that U.S. stocks should perform fairly well over the next couple of decades.

### Price/Earnings Ratio

At the turn of the century, the dot-com madness was reaching its peak and had pushed stock valuations to record levels. Stocks weren't just a little expensive, they were outrageously priced.

The price/earnings ratio (P/E ratio) of stocks and the stock market is a commonly used measure of the current valuation, or cost, of stocks. The P/E ratio divides the price of one share of stock by the earnings produced by the same share.

The ratio provides a basic measure of the price of a stock or, when looking at the ratio across the S&P 500, the market in general. Although it's only a rough measure of value because so many factors can affect the earnings part of the equation, the ratio still provides a quick and relevant indicator of how cheap or expensive a stock or the market may be.

In December 1999, the P/E ratio of the S&P 500 reached 44,[1] which was dramatically higher than its average of around 16.[2] A high price/earnings ratio isn't necessarily bad because companies can sometimes grow fast enough to justify high prices. A company with a high P/E ratio may be worth more than a company with a lower P/E ratio if it can increase its earnings (E) at a much more rapid pace than the company with the lower P/E ratio. If the company's earnings increase, the future P/E ratio will decrease as the denominator increases, assuming that the price stays constant. So, when investors pay more for a given dollar of earnings that a company generates, they are making their investment based on the belief that the company will be able to grow its earnings more rapidly and justify the higher price they are paying for today's earnings.

Throughout the 1990s dot-com craze, investors continually bid up the price/earnings ratios. Expectations for future profit increases seemed boundless. Some pundits talked of a new reality in which historical P/E ratios and other fundamental measures of corporate profitability were no longer relevant or would need to be adjusted.

But around mid-1999, corporate earnings for the companies in the S&P 500 peaked. The news had been so good for so long that investors were slow to acknowledge the earnings peak, and stock prices kept going up until the end of the first quarter of 2000 (different markets, such as the Nasdaq, the S&P 500, and the Dow Jones Industrial Average, reached their highs on different days). Once investors lost confidence in ever-increasing earnings, stock prices began a decline that lasted nearly two years. During the downturn, earnings fell only through the second quarter of 2000, but prices did not start recovering until October 2002.

By this point, equity prices had fallen far enough that P/E ratios reached around the mid to low 20s, or about half of their previous highs. The market itself had fallen by about half in reaching these levels while earnings had returned to similar heights seen before the market plunge. As a result, most of the decline in the P/E ratio resulted from lower stock prices, not changes in earnings.

The ability of both the price (P) and the earnings (E) to move reveals some of the complexity and challenge of using the P/E ratio as a measurement or predictor of all things related to stocks.

Yet, even with the decline in prices during the dot-com collapse, P/E ratios didn't decline to their previous averages. Stocks remained expensive partly because the availability of cheap capital and easy access to home equity loans kept consumers spending and investors confident that the economy would keep moving forward strongly.

The economic and financial collapse starting in 2007 ushered in a very different set of expectations. During this decline, P/E ratios dropped below their historical average as prices declined even faster than earnings.

First investors panicked over the future of the U.S. and world economies, and then longer-term gloom regarding the U.S. and global recoveries set in. Even after the doubling of the S&P 500 by the end of the first quarter of 2012 from its low on March 6, 2009, stocks never reached their long-term average. The P/E ratio remained low because prices did not increase nearly as fast as earnings.

While the P/E ratio is not an all-inclusive or incredibly complex stock market measurement, it continues to provide a quick and meaningful snapshot of the probable direction of the stock market. When valuations are higher than normal, corporate earnings growth must increase faster than normal to justify the higher prices paid by investors. When the P/E ratio is low, expectations are low, and even moderate growth can generate solid stock market returns.

History bears this out. When P/E ratios are low, stock market performance in the following years has been strong, while markets with high P/E ratios usually deliver poor performance in subsequent years. On average, as the P/E ratio increases by 5, expected future returns over the next decade decrease by about 3 percent per year.[3] This isn't a precise prediction, just a strong indicator of likely future trends.

Low P/E ratios also tend to offer somewhat more downside protection. When P/E ratios are low, investors can still earn pretty good returns even if the economy limps along because a lot of the bad news is already built into stock prices. Of course, if confidence increases and earnings also increase, investors can reap rewards as two trends favor them. First, as investors drive up stock prices, P/E ratios increase and often surpass their historical norms because of improving investor confidence.

Second, as earnings increase, unless prices increase at the same rate as earnings, the P/E ratio will fall. So, when earnings go up, to keep the P/E ratio constant, prices must go up by the same amount as earnings. And when sentiment is improving, investors tend to believe that higher P/E ratios for all stocks are justified. The result is an increase in price (P) that outpaces the rise in earnings (E). Both improving profits and improving sentiment drive prices higher. When both occur, a bull market often ensues. Not surprisingly, bull markets nearly always start when valuations are below historical averages.

Of course, prices often take time to improve. Profits do not automatically rise just because P/E ratios are low, and struggling economies don't recover according to a standard script. Investors' tendency, however, is to assume that sideways or downward trends will continue indefinitely rather than for relatively short time periods. This often provides excellent buying opportunities.

While some people will claim accurately that the economy struggled from 2009 through 2012, the stock market essentially doubled over this time frame largely because valuations had been driven down to ridiculously low levels in 2008 and corporate profits, or earnings, had managed to recover nicely, in spite of tepid economic growth.

During this time frame, the downside protection that often accompanies low P/E ratios also was evident. Since valuations were already low, shocks to the economy, bad news, or lack of good news usually had less negative impact on the stock market.

As of mid-2012, P/E ratios continue to hover around 14. These levels are not incredibly low, but they are below the trend, as they have been for the past several years. Historically, when P/E ratios start solidly below historical trends, the ensuing decade has been pretty good for investors.

## Corporate Earnings

In the previous section on valuations, earnings were mentioned several times as a key part of valuations. One of the major reasons that P/E ratios have remained below historical norms in spite of the market's more than doubling in the three years since the 2009 low has been the strength of corporate earnings growth. Earnings more than doubled from the first quarter of 2008 through the end of 2010, and have continued to go higher through the second quarter of 2012, moving well above prerecession levels.[4]

While the economy lagged behind the normal postrecession recovery and unemployment remained stubbornly high, the U.S. private sector adjusted to difficult conditions. In spite of slow corporate revenue growth, corporate earnings, the primary driver of stock prices, remained strong and continued to set new records.

Corporate profits are also helped by low interest rates. In particular, when short-term interest rates are very low, companies can borrow cheaply to fund operations, investment, working capital needs, or any action they believe will move the company forward. The low cost of capital contributes to higher profitability and acts as a tailwind for company actions.

The ongoing uncertainty in the market after the meltdown altered corporate behavior in multiple areas. As of mid-2012, one lingering impact that could further benefit investors remained the incredibly high level of cash on corporate balance sheets.

Lack of confidence in a slow-growing and unstable economy kept investors on the sidelines, and corporations were slow to move forward with new investments, including hiring. While this trend is likely to end at some point, as of this writing, corporate America continues to sit on record amounts of cash.

The cash provides investors two likely benefits. First, the cash provides greater protection against any future slowdown. If domestic or global events were to force the United States back into recession, which I believe is highly unlikely in the near term, corporations have far more resources that they can use to adjust and maneuver.

Second, and I believe this is the likelier event, corporations are sitting on an incredible amount of dry powder that can be employed as the economy picks up. While the timing of new investments remains uncertain, the potential impact on earnings offers investors another reason to believe in the future of stocks.

Corporate earnings recovered strongly after the depths of the recession, and they have continued to climb. Most projections predict further increases, in spite of tepid economic growth, and if the economy were to grow at faster rates in the future, greater earnings increases would probably result. The highly positive impact of earnings on stock market prices suggests that future equity performance should remain strong as earnings continue their upward climb.

## Energy

Like low-cost access to borrowing, the cost of other major economic inputs affects corporate profits. Energy expenses contribute substantially to overall economic costs in nearly any economy, and energy prices have a dramatic impact on personal, corporate, and government decisions.

The United States is undergoing a surprising and largely unexpected energy boom. While we've always had enough energy in the form of oil, coal, and natural gas in the United States to be energy independent, various regulations and restrictions have prevented us from producing enough to meet our domestic needs. Green energy sounds like a wonderful idea, but the technologies remain decades away from having a serious impact on our energy needs in this country. We may eventually replace many or even most of our current energy sources, but the change will not happen over a one- or even a ten-year time period. Regardless of when or if we abandon hydrocarbons as our major energy source, a change of that magnitude will take decades.

In the meantime, the United States has seemingly been given a gift—cheap, abundant, clean-burning natural gas. And we have a lot of it. Moreover, we keep finding more. In 2008, natural gas was $14 per metric cubic foot (MCF). As of mid-2011, the price had plummeted to nearly $2 per MCF, versus $10 in Germany and $16 across most of Asia.[5] According to a December 2011 Congressional Budget Office study, U.S. total energy reserves, which includes natural gas, oil, and coal, exceed all other countries in the world including the Middle East.[6]

Access to cheap energy gives the United States a tremendous cost advantage and fundamentally changes outsourcing logic as U.S. workers become comparatively more attractive. Dow Chemical recently built a plant in Texas that had been slated for China. UPS and FedEx are converting their fleets to natural gas. America will probably be energy independent in the not too distant future (5 to 20 years), with the time frame largely being determined by government policy.

Cheap energy's impact can't be overstated because it affects nearly every part of the economy. Much lower cost inputs can cover a multitude of problems in various sectors of government and the economy. It can also help the United States continue to lead an increasingly integrated and expanding global economy.

Going back to corporate profits, less expensive energy decreases costs for nearly every company in some way. Over the past year, I've attended or spoken at seven different financial conferences. At every conference, several speakers and economists highlighted the potentially major impact that inexpensive natural gas and possible energy independence could have on the United States.

One conference particularly stands out. In May 2012, Fidelity (the big mutual fund company that also runs the second-largest clearing firm in the United States that provides custody of stocks, bonds, private investments, and so on for investors) hosted its major annual conference for senior leaders and owners of firms that it serves. During the conference, multiple economists, market experts, and TV pundits spoke. Without exception, every person cited inexpensive and plentiful natural gas as a likely game-changer for the United States over the next 20 years because of its likely positive impact on corporate profits.

## Inflation

Eventually, inflation is likely to increase above the 2.5 percent average it has posted from 2000 to 2011.[7] Over the past 30 years, inflation has been only slightly higher, at 3.0 percent per year. But in the 10 years previous to this period, 1972 to 1981, inflation averaged nearly 8.5 percent.[8] Many investors, economists, and financial advisors worry that the recent spending and borrowing by the U.S. government during this past recession will cause significant inflation in the future. I agree, and I strongly believe that inflation will rise at some future time. The bigger questions are likely to be the ultimate level that inflation hits and the duration of higher rates.

In the previous section, the positive impact of low interest rates on corporate profits was listed as a current driver of U.S. corporate profits. It seems obvious that higher rates would adversely affect earnings and therefore act as a drag on U.S. stocks.

As with seemingly everything linked to inflation, however, the argument isn't as simple as may be expected. Historically, over time frames of a year or less, inflation has driven profits down because costs increase faster than companies can increase their prices. But over the longer term, companies adjust to different circumstances, and inflation becomes almost a nonfactor.

I like a study that looks at the longer-term impact of inflation on stocks from 1871 up through 2011. This study showed that, surprisingly, future 10-year real (net of inflation) returns were at their highest when inflation was in the highest quintile, or 20 percent of its range. For other quintiles, lower inflation tended to produce slightly better real returns, but not by much. Real returns among the bottom four quintiles remained fairly constant, ranging from 7.1 to 6.5 percent per year.[9]

Essentially, real returns fluctuated little, as overall returns incorporated the effects of inflation. The combination tends to make stocks a pretty good inflation hedge over the longer term, since they provide returns well above inflation regardless of what level inflation reaches. Still, in the short term, corporations would lose the advantage of very cheap capital that they have enjoyed during the last several years.

## Growth of the United States

While the previous sections have addressed several advantages that stocks could enjoy over the coming decades, U.S. equities probably face at least one very significant headwind. Very simply, the United States is no longer an emerging market enjoying the higher annual GDP growth rates of emerging markets. While this is obvious, the simple fact is easy to ignore when analyzing historical market returns and guessing about the future.

Many of the historical return numbers cited for U.S. stocks were generated at a time when the United States was growing at much faster rates than those anticipated for the next 20, 30, or even 50 years. It's simply unlikely that the United States will enjoy the growth rates on a regular basis that were commonly expected 50 or 75 years ago.

Assuming probable future GDP growth rates near or under 3 percent in combination with projected population growth and various other economic trends, many analysts anticipate that real growth rates (growth rates net of inflation) are likely to average no more than 4 to 5 percent versus a historical average of about 6 percent.[10]

After all the reasons listed previously regarding the potential future of U.S. stocks, this may appear pessimistic, but these numbers are probably still pretty good. If inflation were to continue at 2.5 percent, this would put total stock returns at 6.5 to 7.5 percent. Given that inflation is expected to increase, stock returns would probably rise as well, pushing them up closer to historical averages.

Of course, projections of lower growth rates could also be simply wrong. Private enterprise in the United States has a remarkable track record of successfully adjusting to the challenges thrown at it, and as corporate America earns an increasing percentage of its revenues from abroad, growth is likely to become more linked to higher emerging market growth rates than to lower U.S. levels. While earnings may continue at historical rates, some temperance regarding future growth-rate projections may be wise given lower GDP growth rate expectations.

## Volatility

In spite of all this good news, I believe expectations for stocks should be tempered for other reasons. While returns are likely to reach acceptable levels over longer time frames, numerous factors pose potential challenges to stocks that could delay their increase or make them a less desirable investment holding. Stocks as an asset class have a history of large swings, and the future is likely to bring even greater volatility. The rapid rises and falls over the last 20 years make that painfully apparent.

The reasons for increased volatility are numerous, and the complexity of international markets and rapidly advancing technology, among countless other changes, makes exact identification of them impossible. Yet some very basic trends strongly suggest that high volatility will likely plague today's investors for the rest of their lives. Volatility will probably increase rather than decline, even if we occasionally see calmer markets.

Technology certainly plays a major role in creating wider and more frequent market swings. Whether it's enabling an individual investor to change their 401(k) allocation or providing a hedge fund manager with the information needed to place computer-driven million-dollar trades, the ability for a wide range of investors to easily, cheaply, and rapidly make and act on decisions has created an entirely different trading dynamic from what existed only 20 years ago.

In the late 1980s, I worked with Morgan Stanley's proprietary trading desk, where computer algorithms were used to identify trends and execute trades. At the time, these techniques and practices were viewed as highly sophisticated. If nothing else, they were rare.

Today, nearly every hedge fund across the multitrillion-dollar industry does something similar. By some estimates, as of August 2011, some type of computerized trading accounted for 40 to 70 percent of all volume traded on U.S. markets versus only 10 percent a decade earlier.[11]

This represents a small part of the industry change. If you had a 401(k) 20 years ago, you probably remember the difficulties and restrictions on changing your investment and holding allocations. Often changes were limited to once per quarter. Today, most plans allow unlimited reallocations, executable at any time.

Buying and selling nearly any liquid stock investment has grown dramatically easier and cheaper over the past several decades. While none of these changes alone has had a terrific impact, the combination of multiple technology and trading improvements that facilitate dramatically easier, faster, and cheaper trading have combined to create markets that move with lightning speed compared to just a few years ago.

Market moves of greater than 1 percent were highly unusual just a few years ago. Today, they are common. In 2011, there were 35 trading days that ended with moves of at least 2 percent, the most since the 2008–2009 crisis.[12] The three-month historical volatility gauge known as the VIX hit its record high on October 31, 2011. The level was more than double its median during the previous decade.[13] Various other volatility measures place 2011 as at or near the most volatile year in market history.

Does this mean that every year will continue to see record volatility? It's doubtful. Various international events probably contributed to making this year special, and 2012 started off calmer. The greater point is that volatility is likely to remain significantly higher in the future than it's been in the past, regardless of domestic or international events.

For investors, increased volatility usually has a highly negative impact, and future market movements are likely to subject investors to a bumpier ride. If investors had demonstrated a great track record in holding their course through turbulent times, increased volatility might be insignificant. But, the opposite has been true. The 7.85 percent underperformance of equity investors versus the S&P 500 in 2011, mentioned earlier, seems to demonstrate the problem.

Partially because of volatility, stocks can also go out of favor and languish for years, even if their earnings and other fundamentals suggest that they are worth more. It's been said by more than one wise man that stock pricing can remain irrational longer than investors can remain solvent.

When we combine all the various positive and negative influences on stock returns, it seems likely that stocks will perform reasonably well over the next 10 to 20 years, but performance could remain quite rocky. As always, returns are likely to remain unpredictable, with gains possibly starting this year, next year, or in five years. And, the market can always go down regardless of valuations, the economy, or energy prices. Fortunately, the market doesn't tend to remain mispriced for too long, but history provides several examples of long sideways stock markets that pummel investors before shares take off as investors again decide that stocks are the place to be.

## Implication for Stocks

Given all these issues affecting U.S. equities, what are the likely implications for the asset class in individual investors' portfolios? Are stocks worth keeping, or will they disappoint as they did for the first decade of the millennium?

In summary, I believe that the combination of reasonable valuations, expectations of strong future corporate earnings for various reasons, and the likely benefits of cheaper energy all suggest that U.S. stocks should perform fairly well over the next 10 to 20 years. Inflation will probably inflict some damage on stocks on a short-term basis, assuming that it increases at some time over the next few years, but corporations should adjust, making stocks a good long-term hold.

Still, if you are near or in retirement, you need to ask yourself a key question. In spite of my arguments voicing optimism, do you want to place a large percentage of your assets in an investment in which most individual investors have dramatically underperformed and that is subject to many unpredictable domestic and global influences, is likely to experience high levels of volatility for multiple reasons, and can behave irrationally for extended time periods?

As much as I like the stock market, it seems prudent to limit the percentage of assets invested in stocks, especially if you are near or in retirement. More sophisticated investors agree, and more details on their approach will be covered in the next chapter. Understanding the potential challenges offered by this asset class remains the greater point. It can deliver strong, excellent returns and always provides complete liquidity, but its inherent limitations make it a very angular investment.

Stocks are not bad, but they are simply imperfect, as all investments are. Investing with an expectation that your investments will provide strong and consistent performance when all history suggests something else simply doesn't seem wise. Equities do not offer the ideal combination of risk, income, and performance that most investors desire for their retirement portfolio. No single investment does. They seem poorly suited to provide the primary performance element within the traditional 60/40 stock/bond portfolio structure. They probably can contribute value to a portfolio, but their inherent flaws are likely to mean that their overall allocation in any retirement portfolio should be limited.

This assumption marks a major departure from the investment approach employed by a large percentage of individuals. Looking at the other side of the traditional approach provides a second major change.

## Bonds

Years ago, many retirees financed their retirement largely by collecting interest from their bond portfolios. Bonds also provided a relatively safe means to preserve wealth. Bond returns tend to be significantly less volatile than those of stocks, and they have offered a relatively straightforward means of producing income without assuming too much risk. Some people used certificates of deposit (CDs) rather than bonds to achieve similar goals. While CDs are definitely different from bonds, the performance of a five-year CD and a five-year government bond has historically been fairly similar, offering investors a desired combination of income and shield from volatility.

### Recent History

For the last 30 years, bonds have worked especially well, averaging a 9.0 percent annual return. Their performance over this time frame provided investors with an unprecedented bull run in bonds. At one point during the recent market meltdown, 25-year stock returns trailed 25-year bond returns using the traditional S&P 500 and Barclays Capital U.S. Aggregate Bond Index as indicators.

If bonds can provide this type of return, why bother with anything else? The challenge for today's investors is that these returns resulted from a unique set of circumstances. Going back to the late 1970s and 1980s, inflation and interest rates were uncommonly high. The prime rate, the rate that banks have historically charged their best customers, reached its record high of 21.5 percent on December 19, 1980.[14] If you took out a mortgage in the late 1970s or 1980s, you probably remember the ridiculous interest rates you paid.

By comparison, on June 20, 2012, the U.S. prime rate remained at 3.25 percent, its lowest level since October 14, 1955.[15] The 30-year time span ending in 2011 offered bondholders a nearly perfect environment for strong returns, with interest rates starting at record highs and steadily declining to record lows.

A declining-rate environment benefits bondholders because the original rates paid on previously issued bonds become more valuable as rates decrease. When current rates decrease, the principal value of the bonds increases because investors are willing to pay more to get the higher rate on bonds issued with higher rates. Not only are the original bondholders rewarded through enjoying higher yields than those available elsewhere, but their holdings also increase in value.

If the original bondholder keeps the bond until maturity, the value of the bond will decline to the redemption price that is paid to the bondholder at the bond's maturity, but the investor will still continue to enjoy higher interest payments than those available from other bonds with similar risk. As interest rates decline, bondholders have the option of holding their higher-yielding bonds or selling the bond for a premium to investors who are willing to pay more for the higher yield. This has been the environment for bondholders for three decades.

A few years ago I met with a man who was trying to replace various bonds he had purchased from the state of New Jersey near the height of interest rates in the late 1970s through early 1980s. His 25-year bonds, which were starting to mature, all paid more than 20 percent per year. He had bought them believing that rates would probably go down in the future, making government-backed bonds very attractive. Obviously, he was right!

While holding the bonds, he enjoyed the choice of receiving more than 20 percent returns per year, or selling the bonds at a substantial gain that varied over the years depending on the prevailing interest rates and the time left to maturity. This conversation took place around 2005. Since then, rates have gone even lower.

Unfortunately, the conditions that helped bonds so dramatically over the past three decades have created a much more difficult future for bonds. As of the middle of 2012, the Barclays Capital U.S. Aggregate Bond Index's yield remained under 2.6 percent.[16] Obviously, this falls far short of the 9.0 percent annual return generated over the previous 30 years. The 10-year Treasury yield on July 12, 2012, was only 1.5 percent, and even the 30-year Treasury yield was only 2.57 percent.[17]

At these levels of return, bonds start to look much more like return-free risk than risk-free return. When interest rates go up, the opposite dynamic to the one that has been in place for the last 30 years takes effect. If you hold a note paying 1.5 percent, and interest rates go to 3 percent, the value of your bond decreases because it is less desirable.

Many people invest in fixed income through bond mutual funds or similar investment vehicles. The pricing works the same way. When interest yields paid on government securities increase, all the current holdings in a bond fund decline in value, assuming that other characteristics remain the same.

## Looking Forward

After the 2007–2009 financial meltdown, bond rates compressed as investors fled to the perceived safety of bonds. Although interest rates were low, total bond returns including capital gains remained strong, since declining yields increase the value of bonds. Record low rates, however, have turned bonds into primarily a safe place to store funds rather than a means to generate income or returns. In the second quarter of 2012, the Barclays Capital U.S. Aggregate Bond Index provided a total return of 0.30 percent, or approximately 1.2 percent annualized return, which isn't surprising given its total yield of under 2.6 percent.

The ultra-low interest-rate environment presents two challenges. First, interest yields are so low that they provide investors with after-tax yields that lag inflation. Second, bonds carry substantial interest-rate risk. When inflation, or even expectations of inflation, increases, the yields required by investors nearly always rise to compensate investors for the use of their money because it is expected to decline in value.

The fantastic bond performance for the past 30 years resulting from falling interest rates holds a warning for investors over the next couple of decades, as rates appear certain to rise. U.S. government borrowing is at record highs, and many if not most economists expect inflation to increase in the future. Arguments seem to focus on how high inflation may rise and when it will move higher rather than on whether it will rise.

Inflationary environments punish bondholders. Much of the bond bull market of the past 30 years resulted from taming the high inflation of the late 1970s and early 1980s. While I don't believe we'll see inflation levels reach the highs of 30 years ago, average inflation rates higher than the 1.5 percent seen over the period from 2009 to 2011 seem likely.[18]

In past decades, rising interest rates have punished bond investors. At the end of World War II, bond rates were low, and they increased for more than 30 years until this last bull market began in the early

1980s. Bondholders faired poorly over these decades of rising rates. Unfortunately, investors holding bonds today receive very little compensation in the form of yield for assuming substantial interest-rate and inflationary risk.

## What Is Conservative?

Historically, bonds have often been assumed to play the role of the safe, or at least the safer, portion of a portfolio. And during and after the meltdown, bonds delivered safety just as expected. For the five years from 2007 to 2011, returns never dropped below 5 percent and they averaged 6.5 percent. Looking forward, bonds probably will remain much less volatile than stocks, but if interest rates rise, they can also suffer significant losses.

But bond yields well under 3 percent offer little upside and a great deal of potential downside. In this environment, can bonds still be considered a safe investment? And how is a safe investment defined in today's environment? Is it insulation from loss, or is maintenance of purchasing power a more meaningful definition? If inflation flares up, bond values are likely to decline, and their purchasing power could be hit even harder. You may get all your money back, but it may buy much less.

With this altered reality, the old assumptions regarding the value and use of bonds seem not just out of date, but truly dangerous. Bonds have historically been assumed to be a safer investment, but an ultra-low rate environment with a substantial threat of future inflation turns many assumptions upside down.

In the midst of these challenges, the financial services industry is struggling to determine the right recommendations for investors, and for retirees in particular. Can you recommend government bonds as a conservative investment? In 2011 and 2012, various experts and pundits declared that the United States is experiencing a bond bubble similar to that of stocks a few years ago, and that bonds were actually a very risky asset class. Even the old sage Warren Buffett called bonds "among the most dangerous of assets" in early 2012.[19] And these comments all exclude the discussion of recent downgrades of government bonds by the ratings agencies.

## The Purpose for Bonds

I believe U.S. investment-grade bonds still offer value, but the benefits have changed. Bonds have turned into a safe haven for funds rather than an investment. Returns are anemic, and risk is much higher than normal. Yet bonds, particularly shorter-term bonds, still offer complete liquidity and reduced principal risk. But their use probably stops there. Bonds simply don't offer a compelling upside in any area, while they present investors with unusual risks, creating a cloud over the other component of traditional portfolios.

## The Traditional Investments

Combining the likely futures for domestic stocks and bonds provides a somewhat uninspiring projection. Stocks may provide reasonably solid returns over the next 10 to 20 years, yet they are likely to carry substantial risk and heightened volatility. Investors have also managed to woefully underperform stocks and seem to struggle more when volatility is higher.

Bonds also appear to face several challenges. Future returns are likely to be well below historical averages, and very low interest yields offer investors much greater risk than normal, especially when adjusted for dramatically lower return expectations.

If you are in or near retirement, I don't believe these investments are attractive enough to warrant their use for the bulk of your portfolio. Stocks may be an appropriate investment for some of your funds, but depending on this asset class to generate the majority of the future performance of a retirement portfolio seems unwise.

Bonds look worse. They may provide a place for investors to hide, but even their ability to protect investors from risk seems questionable if inflation picks up. And their inability to produce income combined with their poor total return prospects positions them as a very poor component of any retirement portfolio. For government bonds, the phrase reward-free risk rather than the traditional description of risk-free reward seems only too appropriate.

## Much Room for Improvement

After looking at the potential futures of stocks and bonds, it seems that retirement portfolios could benefit tremendously from a design that incorporates a different approach and other types of assets. Hopefully, you are convinced of the need to do something different, and of the dangers of continuing forward with strategies and investments that are unlikely to provide the results that most people want.

The great news is that different strategies that include far more diverse assets have been modeled and implemented very successfully by sophisticated investors over time frames spanning decades. The concepts are not new, and they are highly accessible. Moreover, these investors faced the same challenges associated with stocks and bonds, and they have developed robust approaches to build portfolios that can weather the inevitable storms affecting both asset classes.

In addition, the last decade, and particularly the years since the financial meltdown, has brought far more investment possibilities to individual investors. The realization of the limitations of the traditional investment model has created a rapidly growing group of people who are seeking investments similar to many of those used by much larger institutions. Not surprisingly, the market has responded, and in many cases, the same people who have provided investment opportunities to very large and sophisticated investors are now working directly with individuals.

In the next chapter, the approaches employed by many of the world's most successful investors will be covered, along with different means by which individuals can emulate their strategies.

## 5

# A More Advanced Investment Approach

HAVE YOU EVER WONDERED HOW VERY LARGE INVESTORS MANAGE their portfolios? If they are managing $10 billion, do you think they simply throw approximately $6 billion into stock mutual funds and leave the other $4 billion for bond funds? To make it more personal, if you were handed $10 billion to manage for the benefit of a prestigious university and its students, or maybe you were entrusted with acting on the behalf of 35,000 retirees through a pension fund, would you just cavalierly divide the assets into a 60/40 allocation across equity and bond mutual funds, and then hope for the best? You probably assume that larger, sophisticated investors take a very different approach to investing their funds, and they do.

## Sophisticated Investors' Goals

Just like individuals, institutions strongly dislike volatility and unpredictability, yet they also want strong investment returns over time. In addition, income is usually very important to institutions that are providing operating funds for a college or benefits to pensioners.

For both college endowments and corporate pensions, the demands on these institutional portfolios often strongly resemble

**63**

those of a retiree. They need current income, want future portfolio growth, and seek to avoid volatile and unpredictable performance.

Even their time frames are more similar to retirees' than people may assume. The average college endowment assumes about a 50-year time horizon. In my experience, most people think that this is much longer than their own time horizon. Yet, reality suggests otherwise. If you are a married 60-year-old, you should be planning for at least 30 years, and a 35-year time horizon is statistically more appropriate. If you are a single 65-year old, actuarial tables suggest a shorter time frame, but do you really want to make it likely that you will run out of money when you are 85?

Even if you are 70, if you are in reasonably good health, 20 years is probably a minimum time horizon. Of course, if you're only 50, you should probably be planning for the next 40 years. No one wants to outlive their money.

While all these time frames fall short of 50 years, a portfolio management time frame of at least 10 years tends to make the constraints on portfolios quite similar to those of an endowment. Minimally, realistic assumptions regarding retirement portfolios versus the portfolios of larger institutions create objectives and constraints for individuals that are much more similar to those of institutions than they are different.

Endowments can sometimes face greater constraints than individuals. Most colleges with significant endowments enjoy ongoing alumni donations. The flow of new funds into the school helps add to the funds available from endowment investment returns. Of course, tuition is also a major source of funding, as are research grants and other income streams.

Yet, as a percentage of the overall budget, universities may receive a smaller percentage of their funds through ongoing sources than a retiree who receives social security and possibly other income from pensions or other sources. It's not unusual for retirees to meet a substantial portion or even the majority of their income needs through predictable and effectively guaranteed sources. Portfolio income acts as a supplement, and a one- or two-year interruption may be inconvenient, but not disastrous.

By contrast, college endowments rarely have the luxury of decreasing the amount or delaying the timing of income provided to a school. Regardless of market or economic conditions, their contributions must continue. If they reduce their contributions, the impact tends to be significant, and often highly public. At a minimum, the importance of endowment income contributions to their beneficiaries rivals or exceeds the importance of a retirement portfolio's income to its owner.

## Opportunity

Over the past several decades, many institutions, particularly larger college endowments, have achieved excellent investment success through various stock market and economic conditions. And they have achieved their success in spite of enduring the same investment climate as individual investors. They provide an excellent example of success.

College endowments are particularly interesting for several reasons. As mentioned, their objectives and constrains are very similar to those of individual investors, particularly retirees.

Their success and their different approach to building and managing their portfolios make them particularly interesting. Moreover, the record of these endowments' past actions and plans for the future are easily accessible. Endowments publish their broad investment intentions for the upcoming year and clearly state their percentage targets for various asset classes. No detective work is required.

Access to this information and recognition that the approach taken by endowments differs dramatically from that of the typical investor provides individuals with a fantastic opportunity. The portfolios of typical endowments rarely resemble those of individual investors.

Given their size and their far greater resources, it can be tempting to assume that the success of endowments results from strategies or investments that are unavailable to the average individual investor. Yet my experience and various studies suggest that individuals can duplicate large parts or even all of the actions taken by endowments to achieve dramatically different returns from those of far too many individual investors.

A study by the *Journal of Wealth Management* reaches an incredibly encouraging conclusion. The journal's review of Yale's 20-year performance ending in fiscal year 2007[1] found that Yale's success resulted from its allocation of assets across different investment categories rather than its skill or luck in selecting managers, except for the category of private equity. The authors' analysis of the 10-year data reached the same conclusion.

A quick explanation might help here. David Swensen began managing the Yale endowment portfolio in 1985. He is largely credited with making the first major departures from the traditional portfolio approach and developing what has become known as the endowment approach to investing. After Yale originated the approach, many endowments and institutions copied the strategy and have achieved largely similar results. Some version of the strategy has become standard for nearly all endowments and institutions worldwide. Notably, the success of other endowments and institutions appears to result from the strategies adopted, meaning asset allocation, rather than from the use of particular managers or product specialists.

This represents an incredible opportunity because strategy can be duplicated. If success resulted from relationships or investment managers that were available only to billion-dollar institutions, individual investors might have little hope. But the opposite has consistently been the case. Historically, it's been the choice of asset classes, not particular managers, that has made the primary difference.

By asset class, I mean stocks, bonds, or something else. Essentially, endowments obtained their strong returns because they targeted investments other than the traditional asset classes of stocks and bonds. Many of the larger and more famous endowments normally invest not just a portion, but the majority of their portfolios in holdings other than U.S. stocks and bonds.

The recent economic and stock market challenges have created even more opportunity for individual investors. At the turn of the century, the availability of various nonstandard investments to individuals was more limited. If you wanted to adopt strategies similar to those of endowments, either you had less choice or you needed to have enough assets to look like a small institution. Many very wealthy investors began adopting similar strategies years ago because they had greater access to a much broader range of investments than were widely available to individuals with lesser means.

Today, many of the same investments that were created and managed by the professionals working with large institutions are available to individual investors. Availability to individuals has been increasing for many years, but the financial meltdown and a second stock market crash in the same decade accelerated demand by individual investors who were looking to diversify away from the stock market. Most individuals still haven't made the shift, but there have been enough early adopters to expand investment demand rapidly.

The result has been a vast increase in investment possibilities since the meltdown. Where there may previously have been one or two options available to individuals in a particular investment sector, there may now be more than 20, with the numbers continuing to expand. In addition, new investment options are becoming available across new categories.

Not only has availability increased, but the growth of the market continues to attract larger and more sophisticated firms offering investment possibilities. And more competition among investment managers seeking to attract capital also seems to be steadily improving investment quality. Fees are generally decreasing, and product structures are continually evolving to better match the needs of individual investors. Because so much of the new demand originates from investors who are in or near retirement, many of the investments are designed specifically to meet the needs of people who are focused on retirement.

## Key Differences

Given the intellectual capital that multibillion-dollar endowments can attract, it seems reasonable to expect that their investment approaches would be well thought out. Thinking and planning certainly don't guarantee success, but endowments' investments should be driven by solid research and well-considered expectations. If managers can increase the return on a $10 billion portfolio by only

1 percent, they earned an extra $100 million. That provides a lot of incentive.

The departure by David Swensen and then nearly all other endowments from the typical model originated with the same realizations that have already been covered. The traditional stock and bond model doesn't work very well on a fairly frequent basis, and it often fails to provide investors their desired income and returns with acceptable volatility.

## Performance Assets

To combat the inadequacies of stocks, endowments broadly diversify the assets that they expect to provide strong performance. When diversifying, they strive to include assets that have high performance expectations and also have low performance correlation with one another. Reduced cross-correlation is critical, since if all the new assets behaved in the same way as U.S. stocks, there would be no point in adding them. Investors would simply get the same performance, but from different assets. Instead, different assets are expected to contribute to overall performance, but at different times and in different ways.

When correlations are reduced, various high-performing assets in a portfolio hopefully contribute differently over time and smooth the overall portfolio returns. This is simply another version of not putting all your eggs in one basket. If we refer back to modern portfolio theory, which discussed the trade-off between using stocks and bonds to maximize return versus risk, this approach seeks to fundamentally alter the expected portfolio performance by including far more variables to lessen the impact of inevitable stock volatility. In this way, if U.S. stocks have a bad year, but another asset performs well, the portfolio may still do quite well in spite of the misstep by stocks.

Endowments generally diversify across two main characteristics. First, they diversify by sector. Rather than just buying U.S. stocks, endowments add stocks from other developed markets, such as Germany, Australia, and Switzerland. They also add exposure to stocks from emerging markets, such as China, India, and Brazil. These changes are fairly basic, and they are easy to implement, since numerous means to diversify across these markets have existed for many decades.

In addition, endowments add exposure to less common assets, such as real estate, private equity in companies that do not trade on an exchange, commodities such as oil and gas, absolute return investments that seek performance independent of stock market returns, various high-return debt instruments, and frequently other types of assets with high performance expectations. As mentioned, this is not as difficult for an individual investor to duplicate as it may sound, given the rapid development of new investments.

Second, in an effort to provide more stability, greater return, and decreased correlation, endowments diversify by targeting investments that are less liquid. Investments such as real estate and private equity are excellent examples. Investors hope to earn extra performance from these assets because illiquid assets offer a potential return premium. Investments that require a longer commitment with less access to the invested funds must offer a premium to attract funds.

In the previous list of performance-oriented investments, domestic and international stocks trade on exchanges and are 100 percent liquid. The liquidity provides desirable flexibility, but it also brings with it high volatility. In addition, stock markets across the globe often move in tandem, resulting in higher performance correlations than may be desired, especially in down markets. By adding illiquid assets, endowments seek to secure much greater diversification through differences in both sector and investment type.

By fundamentally altering the portfolio design to include highly diversified assets, endowments hope to combine various assets in a manner that emphasizes their strong benefits while minimizing their shortcomings. All of the high-performance assets seek high returns over time. Like stocks, they have attractive average annual returns. But the lack of correlation of their returns results in overall performance across the portfolio that is smoother and less driven by only the single performance asset of U.S. stocks.

The hope is that in years when U.S. stocks suffer losses, other assets will contribute gains, lessening the impact of the stocks' poor performance. For instance, real estate returns tend to lag stock market returns. Stock investors often anticipate changes in the economy, and stocks frequently rise or fall around six months before the economy improves or declines.

Different variables drive real estate returns. Layoffs usually began occurring well into a recession, and hiring often lags a recovery. As companies lay off workers over time, they can release space only after their leases expire. Office vacancy rates may see little change until a recession has been underway for many months or even years. Similarly, occupancy rates may recover only months or years after an economic recovery, long after the stock market has bounced back up.

Many of the additional assets can also offer other attributes. Some assets may target higher returns than other performance assets, but also carry with them higher volatility. Yet, when these assets are added to the portfolio, their low performance correlation with other assets in the portfolio could decrease the portfolio's total volatility while increasing its total return.

In the long term, the average returns of all the performance assets in an endowment's portfolio may be very strong, but these returns are usually generated at different times and in different ways. The highly diversified portfolios of endowments have produced consistently strong returns with much lower volatility over extended time frames, and the strategy is widely viewed as unparalleled in providing the best risk-adjusted returns over any reasonable time frame.

For some investors, this can be a difficult concept to grasp quickly. If you have six major performance assets in your portfolio rather than just U.S. stocks, the chance of something losing value in any given year goes up. Yet, if U.S. stocks suffer a setback, your portfolio has at least some chance to increase in value if other assets more than cover the losses.

Different endowments set different return targets for the performance component of their portfolio. Just like individuals, endowments differ from one another significantly. Some may seek higher total returns and add more assets with greater return potential. Most endowments that are seeking outsized returns target assets with higher expected performance than stocks, but with volatility or loss potential lower than that of the market. At a minimum, the correlation of these assets with stocks must be low in order for them to warrant consideration and eventual inclusion. Other endowments may target lower returns and much lower volatility by focusing on much lower cross-correlation and more stable returns on additional assets.

Regardless, the primary goal remains consistent—to target high overall returns with a reduced possibility of loss from these assets.

## Fixed Income

This category tends to be simpler. Similar to their approach with performance assets, endowments diversify their holdings in order to reduce their exposure to any particular fixed-income category. They may add international holdings or specific types of fixed income that offer more attractive expected returns versus risk. Yet, these changes usually have minimal impact, as it's not their major action.

The anticipated results of the altered performance side of the portfolio free endowments to choose an entirely different approach. Remember that the original purpose of bonds was to reduce our overall portfolio risk by diversifying into an asset class that has low correlation with stocks. Yet, this has already been done on to the performance asset side of the portfolio through adding various additional noncorrelated assets. If we believe that the performance assets are significantly more stable because of the diversification across multiple lower-correlation holdings, bonds become less necessary and less useful.

Bonds have always had lower expected returns, so after endowments altered the performance side of the portfolio and lowered its expected volatility and risk, they generally sought to increase the overall portfolio return by reducing the amount of lower-performing fixed income in their portfolios. They started this practice decades ago based on lower return expectations for bonds. Over the last 30 years, bonds have done surprisingly well, yet endowments' total returns were improved by their emphasis on higher-performing assets.

In today's environment of ultra-low rates, the de-emphasis of bonds appears to make more sense than ever. With yields on higher-quality fixed income hovering around 2 to 3 percent, and even lower for high-quality government bonds, decreasing bond allocations appears even more likely than normal to increase total portfolio returns.

Of course, there is no guarantee that this will continue to work. All performance assets could decline for an extended time period, making investments in ultra-conservative bonds attractive. Endowments, however, are betting differently.

As of the end of 2010, the average exposure to bonds of 842 colleges and universities was only 13.0 percent plus another 4.0 percent in cash.[2] The superendowments of Yale, Harvard, and Stanford had even less exposure by mid-2011 (endowment fiscal years are July 1 to June 30), at 9.0 percent for bonds and cash.[3]

## Overall Portfolio

In mid-2011, the average allocations across the superendowments of Yale, Harvard, and Stanford illustrated the greater emphasis on highly diversified performance assets and their de-emphasis of fixed income. Figure 5.1 illustrates their average allocations to distinctive asset classes.

Within the category of public equities, endowments tend to allocate around one-third each to U.S. stocks, foreign developed market stocks, and emerging market stocks, although allocations can vary significantly. Harvard's target was exactly one-third to each category, whereas Yale invests more in foreign markets than in the United States, although neither Stanford nor Yale provides exact breakdowns for the July 2011 fiscal year.

**Figure 5.1**   Average Target Allocation for Yale, Harvard, and Stanford (July 2011)

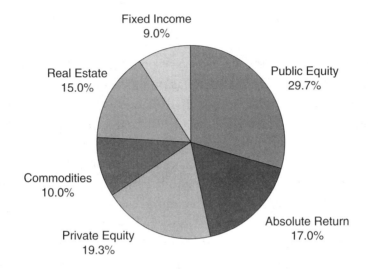

*Sources:* Yale Endowment Report for 2011; Harvard University Financial Report for 2011; Stanford Management Company Report for 2011.

The exact numbers are not nearly as important as the concept of wide diversification across multiple different asset classes. The endowments themselves often pursue substantially different allocations. For instance, for 2011, Yale targeted an exceptionally high allocation to private equity (34 percent), while Harvard and Stanford each aimed for only 12 percent. Private equity allocations across the 842 colleges and universities average only 10.7 percent.[4]

Even with the large differences in allocations, the 12-year performance of the respective endowments during the terrible stock market years of 2000–2011 varied little. Yale, Harvard, and Stanford's net annual returns were 12.14, 10.09, and 10.42 percent, respectively, versus the S&P 500 index's negative return of 0.82 percent.

## Advantages

The strategy employed by endowments offers several potential advantages. Some of them are quite obvious, while others take a bit more effort to appreciate.

Past performance jumps out as an obvious benefit. Over any reasonable time frame and nearly every possible combination of circumstances, the portfolio design has provided superior performance compared with every other widely utilized portfolio structure. It's not perfect, but it's better. Certain asset classes may outperform for short periods, but nothing seems capable of delivering the model's combination of performance and acceptable volatility.

The solid design positions probability on the side of the investor through accounting for inevitable market and economic problems and providing more contributors to success. Greater upside potential makes success more likely and lessens dependence on fickle stock market returns. Reducing dependence on poorer-performing bonds also increases returns expectations. While this hasn't been discussed explicitly, endowments also actively control their fees. You will not see a mutual fund in an endowment's portfolio.

All these performance characteristics result from mathematics, statistics, and probability. Good planning and solid design have produced somewhat predictable results that are potentially available to anyone.

Many of the additional investments also provide significant interest income. For instance, real estate often provides around half of its total return through regular income, and the rental incomes alone have historically been near the interest payments for investment grade bonds. As of 2012, they are generally much higher. Other investments, particularly those focused on alternative debt investments, also provide ample income. If you are in or near retirement, higher income and less dependence on liquidating assets to meet income needs can be highly attractive.

The elegance of the design, however, potentially masks a key element that I believe contributes tremendously to investor success. Not only has success become more likely because of a better portfolio design, but in my experience, the likelihood that investors can successfully manage their more diversified portfolio increases dramatically. Less dependence on U.S. stocks and other volatile assets provides a tremendous emotional advantage.

When U.S. stocks are the only performance asset in a portfolio, the likelihood that investors will panic during crashes or even pullbacks remains unacceptably high. This is true even for professionals. Right before and shortly after the U.S. stock market bottomed in early March of 2009, I spent considerable time convincing multiple financial professionals across the United States to stay with their clients' equity holdings. While they acknowledged that the incredibly low valuations made liquidations probably unwise, they felt their clients' pain acutely and were crumbling under the weight of yet more losses after the 37 percent decline of 2008.

Earlier, the terrible underperformance of investors in both equities and bonds was addressed in various ways, particularly the tendency to perform particularly badly during periods of higher volatility.

The inclusion of far more asset classes helps investors do the right thing at the right time. Greater diversification both lessens fear when problems occur and decreases greed when temptations to chase assets that have already increased in value arise.

As well as diversification, having illiquid assets in the portfolio provides a couple of additional benefits. Partly because they are illiquid and often difficult to value, their exact worth often remains opaque. Values don't tend to move as quickly, and specific data often remain sparse. Valuing these investments can be a bit like estimating the worth of your house. Its value may have changed, but any valuation is always an estimate until you actually sell it. For these illiquid assets, correlation with other assets tends to remain low during even the worst markets.

In addition, even if you want to sell illiquid assets, there is little or no market for them, so you must ride out the storm. Any investor obviously needs to understand this well before adding these assets to a portfolio, but if you make that decision, the discipline forced by the investment's structure can provide tremendous benefit. When investors know that they have no options, they tend to fret less over an asset's value, especially when its value varies less because of limited pricing information.

Less volatility and fewer opportunities to make mistakes result in less anxiety and make investor sabotage less likely. Unlike the stock and bond approach, which seems to prey on investor fallibility, the structure of the endowment model investment approach lessens the impact of individual assets on the portfolio, making successful management more likely during both good and bad markets and economies.

## Adjustments for Individuals

You may be thinking that many of these investments are not appropriate for you, or that you should not limit your safer investments, such as bonds, to only 10 percent of your portfolio. Or, if you have already retired, you may be thinking that illiquid investments are inappropriate for you, although I would point out that few people ever need a major portion of their portfolio liquid over any time period less than several years. These issues may all be valid. Even endowments took a while to realize that investing a portion of a portfolio in illiquid assets offered substantial benefits and not just inflexible inconvenience.

Yet in my experience, adjustments for individual needs usually present limited challenges. The relatively recent tremendous expansion of different investment possibilities for individuals that mimic many of the same investments that endowments use helps investors create well-structured and widely diversified portfolios.

Still, individuals' needs and preferences must always be taken into account as well. For instance, even if you want to maintain a much larger allocation to bonds or other safer investments such as annuities, you can still adopt many of the principles discussed here for the performance side of your portfolio quite easily. Even if you limit your more performance-oriented assets to 50 percent of your portfolio, it seems wise to diversify them away from only U.S. stocks.

You can also compromise. As mentioned, few endowments follow the exact same model, and your portfolio will undoubtedly differ from an institution's. If we take an investor who currently has a standard 60 percent stock and 40 percent bond portfolio, we might decide to implement many of the principles for performance assets and increase the total percentage of performance assets in the portfolio from 60 to 75 percent. The overall portfolio would probably have greater performance potential and lower expected volatility.

In the next chapter, various specific investments and means of including them will be covered. The information will help you make specific allocation and investment decisions. Regardless, it is extremely helpful to think in terms of portfolio success rather than looking only at a particular asset class or individual investments such as stocks or bonds.

As we go through the next section, you may want to note how particular types of investments are available to individuals. Investments such as stocks can be added to a portfolio in nearly countless ways. Some may be better than others, but options exist that will suit nearly any investor preference.

For many of the investments other than stocks that endowments target, the means by which they are available are limited. Most direct investments must be purchased through a registered financial professional and are difficult or impossible to access for someone who is seeking to do everything on their own. This part of the industry is rapidly evolving, and new investment opportunities and means of accessing them will certainly multiply, but to really copy the approach of an endowment, you will probably need to work with a financial professional for at least some of your investments.

While I believe that financial professionals can offer tremendous value, not all investors like working with a professional. It's not a coincidence, however, that investors with more money are much more likely to use financial advisors. Like professional athletes, wealthier individuals recognize the value of expertise and seek it out. As with seemingly everything else in life, the world of finances has gotten increasingly complex, and a good advisor, like any good coach, can offer tremendous value. I will highlight areas that generally require the help of a financial professional versus those that can be accessed independently by individuals.

# 6

# Specific Investments

THIS CHAPTER PROVIDES INFORMATION ON SPECIFIC POTENTIAL investments that can be used to create portfolio designs similar to those that are usually employed by endowments and larger investors. My goal is to provide you with enough information to help you determine how you may want to move forward with this concept. A single chapter will not turn you into an expert on all these different investments, but even a brief explanation of various possibilities can help you determine which investments are of high interest to you and how you may be able to include them in your portfolio.

## Equities

Many of the good and bad characteristics of stocks have already been covered. Like most investments, stocks tend to be angular. They offer solid long-term performance potential and can be sold at any time, but their liquidity and performance potential also make them a volatile asset class, prone to unpredictable moves and cycles.

Nearly all investors, including endowments and institutions, still include a substantial amount of stocks in their portfolio, as the positive characteristics of stocks offer several excellent benefits. Larger investors also make various key choices that help them get the most from this broad category while minimizing some of its less attractive characteristics.

First, they diversify away from only U.S. stocks into various international markets. Second, their investment vehicles provide very efficient access to their targeted investments so that their performance closely tracks the markets they are in, and they minimize their investment costs. Fundamentally, these two choices simplify where and how they invest.

## Which Markets

If you are in or near retirement, most likely you began investing in some way decades ago, whether it was through a 401(k) or on your own through various different investment vehicles. Assuming that you put some of your funds into stocks, you most likely bought U.S. stocks, whether you purchased them directly or through a mutual fund or other investment vehicle. Up until just a few years ago, the value of the U.S. stock market dwarfed that of nearly every other market in the world.

The last few decades have been steadily changing global finances and redistributing global wealth, to the benefit of much of the planet. While the U.S. market has enjoyed solid growth over the past 50 years, markets outside the United States have expanded even more rapidly.

In 1989, the Berlin Wall fell, and my wife and I had the opportunity to travel through much of Eastern Europe during the summer of 1990. The countries' economies were a complete mess. In 1992, we moved to Budapest, Hungary, and lived there for nearly two years. During our stay, the country underwent rapid change, including the slow development of financial markets. My wife, Carol, helped some of the first financial professionals in the country earn their securities licenses. Similar changes and developments were happening all over the region.

We moved to Hong Kong in 1993, when China was rapidly opening up its economy. Hong Kong boomed, as much of China's trade and development was funneled through the city-state. Southeast Asia continued its rapid entry into the global economic scene, partly fueled by China's rise. Around the globe, countries that had been isolated from the world for decades were actively engaging in economic reform.

In 1980, there were fewer than 25 countries that actively participated in the global economic system, and most of the planet suffered from anemic growth rates. In 2007, 124 countries grew faster than 3 percent per year. Even after the financial meltdown, in 2012, 90 countries continue to enjoy growth greater than 3 percent.[1]

In 1970, inflation exceeded 10 percent in the United States, and countries such as Brazil and Peru suffered from inflation greater than 2,000 percent. A total of 35 countries were suffering from hyperinflation. In 2009, the number of countries suffering from hyperinflation dropped to zero when Zimbabwe dollarized its economy.[2]

This incredible generation of wealth across the planet has largely been ignored by many in the United States because of recent problems with our economy. The U.S. stock market earned only 0.41 percent per year over the 11-year period running from December 31, 1999, through December 31, 2010. Annual returns for the 12 years including 2011 improved a bit, rising to 0.55 percent. The returns of developed foreign markets were fairly similar, with annualized 11- and 12-year performances over the same time periods of 1.76 percent and 0.17 percent, respectively.

Emerging stock markets' returns differed more significantly. During the first 11 years of the new millennium, annual returns averaged over 10 percent. However, the uncertainty of global markets punished the stocks of emerging markets even though their economies dramatically outperformed those of developed markets. Emerging markets lost more than 20 percent in 2011, bringing their annual returns over the previous 12 years to only 4 percent. By the end of 2011, emerging market stocks were largely viewed as highly undervalued, as investors had fled to safety, often ignoring under-lying economic fundamentals in favor of security at all costs.

Statistics can tell other stories as well. From 2000 to 2009, U.S. stocks lost value and foreign developed market stocks gained about 1 percent per year, while emerging market stocks grew at around 10 percent annually.

So, what do all these statistics mean, and how can they be used to create a more predictable portfolio with a greater chance of smoother ongoing success?

Today, most endowments and more sophisticated investors spread their equity allocations across domestic and foreign markets, with foreign markets usually receiving the majority of the funds. Investing the majority of an equity allocation in non-U.S. markets more closely mirrors the relative sizes of equity markets across the globe.

The advantages of this are fairly obvious. If you had spread your equity investments evenly across U.S. stocks, foreign developed market stocks, and emerging market stocks from 2000 to 2009, your annualized return would have been plus 3 percent rather than minus 1 percent. A gain of only 3 percent per year isn't very strong, but it results in a total 10-year gain of 35 percent rather than a loss of 10 percent.

Including a few more years of data reveals even more value from diversification. In 2010, most global markets gained, with interna-tional markets, particularly emerging markets, enjoying a strong year. The diversification across stocks would have helped again.

But the following year, with all the different threats presented by earthquakes, government debt downgrades, sovereign debt defaults in Europe, and much more, saw investors once again flee toward safety. One could easily argue that investors' actions in 2011 were foolish if you maintained a longer view, but any such argument is completely hypothetical. Actual returns in 2011 punished investors holding foreign stocks and slightly rewarded investors in the market that was perceived as the safest, the United States. Had all your equities been invested internationally and evenly split across foreign developed and emerging markets in 2011, you would have lost nearly 20 percent. You might have been consoled at the end of a terrible year by the idea that your holdings had great potential because of their low valuations, as economic growth had remained fairly strong in 2011 in spite of the stock market performances. But this would not change the dismal performance of 2011.

By contrast, the United States managed to move forward about 3 percent with dividends. Equity returns across the globe were fairly dismal, but including the United States in a percentage equal to those of emerging markets and developed markets would have reduced your equity losses to 11 percent from more than 18 percent. Neither number is good, but diversification helped defray losses. Over the 12-year period ending in 2011, your equities would have enjoyed much greater success if you had diversified globally, and you would have experienced less volatility and fewer losses. Including more diversified investments also would have smoothed your equity and total portfolio annual returns, illustrating a benefit of intelligent portfolio design.

Perfection is elusive, but improvement can be pretty straight-forward and predictable. Much of the discussion of international stocks has focused on the faster-growing emerging markets. They offer more upside potential and lower correlation with U.S. stocks. You might be wondering whether including stocks from developed foreign markets really offers any benefit.

Nearly all very large investors include developed market stocks in their equity allocations, even though these stocks have limited impact on long-term performance. Their primary benefit in a port-folio has historically been smoothing annual returns. Equities from developed nations offer investors more ways to participate in global growth and constantly evolving economies.

Many developed nations don't enjoy the growth rates of the United States, given that many countries' economic models assume much greater government control. Yet, globally, developed markets have performed fairly well compared to the United States. Moreover, developed markets include more than just the problem economies of Europe. Singapore now enjoys a higher economic output per person than the United States, along with vastly stronger growth rates. Its stock market performance has been much greater than the United States' over the past decade plus, and it has even surpassed the average emerging market.

Equity markets have obviously struggled in recent years, and they now appear to offer strong upside potential. As endowments learned long ago, diversification across various global markets can help investors enjoy greater upside potential with less likelihood of loss during the inevitable pullbacks. Diversification across various markets can even make the entire equity portfolio less volatile.

## How to Invest

Earlier, I excoriated mutual funds for numerous reasons. So, as you may expect, they are not my favorite means of investing in stocks. Of course, exceptions exist, and some mutual funds are excellent. The greater point is securing efficient and effective investment in whatever asset class you are targeting. Numerous opportunities exist to accomplish this.

Many individuals who are investing in the stock market assume that they must try to outperform the market if they are to be successful. Whether it's trying to find highly rated mutual funds or a brilliant stock picker, individuals seem addicted to seeking star managers. This seems to be the automatic first response of all individual investors, since we all naturally strive for success.

With stocks, however, the greater goal should probably be achieving performance that is aligned with the stock market's. When most people analyze the market's past and look toward its future, they nearly always focus on the broad market. Yet, when they invest, most investors chase investments that promise something substantially different from the overall stock market. For their equity investments, endowments generally target returns that mimic the market. When they seek something different, they use completely different strategies, such as hedge funds, which will be covered later in this chapter.

Furthermore, most people should probably focus on avoiding significant underperformance rather than targeting significant outperformance. Finding meaningful and consistent outperformance is hard, and chasing it often results in returns that are far below the general market's. If you can maintain performance reasonably close to your targeted indexes, your total returns from equities will probably turn out fairly strong over time and contribute positively to your portfolio.

Fees strongly influence choices as well, as they can severely affect expected returns. Again, you will pay fees to invest, as they are impossible to avoid. All the previous market performance statistics excluded fees, so they should probably be considered optimistic. And high fees are probably the most predictable indicator of future underperformance.

With this backdrop, what makes the most sense for an individual investor? Books have been written on the topic, and the complexity of individual situations removes the possibility of there being a single solution that fits everyone. In addition, approaches that can work well for domestic equities may be inappropriate for international stocks, particularly in emerging markets. Regardless, a few basic guidelines can simplify the decision.

A first major decision will be whether to manage your own equity portfolio or work with some type of advisor. Some people may be well served by managing their own equity portfolio. It has become dramatically easier for individuals to invest in stocks, mutual funds, or exchange-traded funds that seek to duplicate the performance of equity indexes.

Yet I believe that this approach remains highly inappropriate for many, if not most, individuals. Given my emphasis on keeping fees low, advising against going it alone may seem inconsistent.

My reasoning is very simple. Most people are their own worst enemies. The fees that a competent financial professional charges to manage a stock portfolio can be one of the highest-return investments an individual can make. Adviosry fees usually hover around 1.0 percent of assets per year, which may seem high. But the dismal returns that individuals earn on their own highlight the potential value of professional help. The value of fees may not even be tied to a professional's advice on exactly how or where to invest. Instead, it may be derived more from helping you stay on track through various market and economic ups and downs.

Next, what type of strategy should you target? The previous section emphasized the value of diversifying internationally, so, hopefully, international diversification is assumed. This goes beyond that assumption.

When you consider your strategy for the United States, you will have choices ranging from small-capitalization (cap) growth stocks to large-cap value stocks. Growth stocks have higher price/earnings ratios because investors believe their earnings will grow faster, while value stocks have lower price/earnings ratios because of lower growth expectations.

In addition, the market can be divided into various sectors, such as technology, real estate, energy, industrial, and so on. Historically, investors have been able to earn somewhat higher returns with some different strategies. For example, value stocks have historically out-performed growth stocks.[3] Even though growth stocks may grow faster than value stocks, the price premium paid for growth stocks seems to result in subpar gains over time. If you need income from your portfolio, value stocks may also be attractive because they tend to have higher dividend yields.

Various other strategies also exist that may combine different sectors in a manner that makes future outperformance more likely. For instance, you may start with a basic position following the S&P 500 and then add other holdings that more closely follow sectors with higher expected performance but higher volatility. Your overall performance may be a bit better, and the diversification may offset the increased riskiness of the different sectors.

Remember, however, that different sectors within the U.S. stock market usually have high correlations with the general market. You can get some benefits from diversifying, but they will be limited. The difference will resemble driving down the highway in different lanes rather than taking a different road. The view and the time it takes to get somewhere may be slightly different, but the destination will be pretty much the same.

International investing can present more challenges, since you have fewer options. It can be difficult, expensive, or even impossible to invest in individual securities in many countries. So, adopting a strategy targeting particular types of stocks or sectors may be nearly impossible.

It can be extremely helpful to remember the focus of investing in equities. You want performance that fairly closely mirrors the performance of the general market and rarely trails it by a significant amount for a long period of time. Yet, don't expect perfection. Earlier, we mentioned that nearly every strategy or approach will underperform at some time.

Value stocks can illustrate both of the points just mentioned. The outperformance offered by this sector over time might be enough to pay for all the fees associated with following the strategy. But these stocks don't always outperform. As a category, they struggled in 2007. Any additional outperformance could be a great bonus, but it will nearly always come at the price of deviations from the market over time, including underperformance. Expecting to beat the returns of the stock market by several percentage points a year is probably unrealistic. It's possible, but significant outperformance is much, much less common than large underperformance resulting from various practices ranging from overtrading to chasing hot mutual funds.

Financial professionals often target specific strategies based on their research and experience. Many different approaches can get you to your destination. As mentioned, an emphasis on value stocks for U.S. equities can work well for investors who are seeking income.

Finally, your choice of investment vehicle can have a major impact on your success, partly because fees vary dramatically across different approaches. If you have a portfolio of any size, I believe mutual funds tend to be a poor choice for the multiple reasons already outlined. Some advisors still like mutual funds because of the diversification benefits they offer. They can make sense, but if you implement a strategy that uses mutual funds, make sure you understand the fees extremely well.

In most situations, I prefer separately managed accounts that employ one of a couple of different options. For investments in the United States, many strategies involve the use of separately managed accounts to create a portfolio of individual stocks. Each individual investor's account is completely separate, and no previous holdings can affect another investor's taxes. Fees for these accounts usually range from around 0.50 to 1.50 percent, depending on the type of strategy chosen and the costs of managing and maintaining it. This may seem high if you aren't familiar with typical industry fees, but the costs of these many of these types of accounts are well below those of many other approaches, including mutual funds.

Other separately managed account options use exchange-traded funds rather than stocks. Exchange-traded funds, or ETFs, as they're generally called, usually seek to recreate the performance of a specific index, such as the S&P 500 or the Morgan Stanley Capitalization Index of Europe, Asia, and the Far East (MSCI EAFE). Fees are low partly because there is no strategy and trading is limited because the ETF only mimics a fairly static index. The advantages of ETFs are primarily cost and low or nonexistent taxes.

For domestic equity portfolios, ETFs can provide a cost-efficient means to create excellent diversification with minimal cost. Outside of the United States, ETFs can be one of the best means to invest in foreign markets or regions at limited cost because there are numerous ETFs that target regions, countries, and even specific sectors for more developed countries.

## Recap

Even a portfolio that emphasizes other types of performance assets will normally still contain stocks. And, when domestic and foreign stocks are treated as a single category of assets, they are likely to remain one of your largest holdings. Success in this category remains very important, even if the role of equities diminishes.

Fortunately, a solid approach can be very simple. The major components will generally include strong diversification across global markets, using effective and efficient investments to secure exposure. A financial professional can make this process much easier by helping you to implement solid strategies as well as helping you stay on track. In my experience, professionals make better performance more likely, but this is one area of investing that remains quite open to dedicated do-it-yourselfers. Next, we will go through many of the newer and more innovative investments that endowments routinely employ to improve their returns while reducing portfolio volatility.

## Alternatives

Performance investments other than stocks have been instrumental in the past success of endowments. While stocks struggled during the first decade plus of the new millennium, endowments used alternatives to improve their returns and buffer their portfolios against the market's volatility.

Interest both by institutions and increasingly by individual investors continues to fuel rapid growth in the alternatives. In 2011, assets invested in real estate, private equity, commodities, hedge funds, and infrastructure reached a record $6.5 trillion, according to a recent report from McKinsey & Company, a highly respected management consulting firm. The reasons are pretty simple. As investors increase their allocation to alternative asset classes, returns increase and volatility declines.[4] The combination results in improved risk-adjusted returns.

Investors have noticed. Alternative assets grew at a 14.2 percent compound annual growth rate from 2005 through 2011. That compares to 1.9 percent growth for nonalternative investments. Retail alternative assets and strategies have grown by 21 percent annually since 2005 and now stand at about $700 million, according to the same report.[5] The report assumes a quite limited perspective of alternatives, since many categories are much larger than $700 million by themselves. Regardless, growth and interest are high.

The alternatives category gets its name from its fairly obvious role in portfolios. Investments other than stocks and bonds are called alternatives because they provide an alternative to traditional stocks and bonds. What the name lacks in originality it makes up for in clarity.

Many different alternatives can provide different performance characteristics that can greatly enhance various types of portfolios. While all these alternative assets can potentially improve a portfolio, the investments that are most commonly used by endowments and are also most widely available to individual investors will be covered first.

## Real Estate

While real estate as an investment asset for individual investors remains a relatively new concept, investing in real estate predates almost every other type of investment. Many people have not added real estate to their portfolios partly because they own a house and therefore consider themselves to be investing in real estate already. A house, however, bears little resemblance to most direct real estate investments. In fact, most professionals would argue that a house really isn't an investment, but rather is a forced savings plan, since ownership, maintenance, and mortgages force individuals to put money into an asset that generally offers very limited returns after expenses.

When endowments buy real estate and categorize it as a separate asset class, they specifically target direct ownership in commercial real estate. The primary real estate sectors include commercial office properties, industrial properties such as warehouses, retail properties such as stores, and multifamily properties (apartments). Additional classes such as hospitality (hotels), medical buildings, and special-use facilities also exist, but they tend to receive less focus given the limited size of the markets.

Direct real estate ownership differs dramatically from ownership of traded real estate investment trusts (REITs). Like direct real estate investments, traded REITs can be excellent investments, and most investors, including institutions, hold traded REITs in their stock portfolios.

Traded REITs' performance and volatility, however, strongly resemble those of stocks and frequently are more highly correlated with the stock market than with real estate values. The reason is simple. Traded REITs are stocks. For this reason, endowments and institutions view traded REITs as an equity investment that can enhance particular stock strategies rather than as an investment in real estate.

Just as endowments target direct investment in real estate, individual investors can do the same using nontraded REITs. These investments pool investors' funds into a common fund. Managers of the fund then buy institutional-quality real estate on behalf of the investors. Nontraded REITs usually specialize according to industry, geography, management style, and even more additional characteristics, providing investors with ample choice. Most investors adding real estate to their portfolio spread their funds across at least two or three different offerings.

This investment structure offers both strong positives and potential negatives. On the plus side, direct investment in real estate has little correlation with stocks or nearly any other investments. Most commonly available nontraded REITs also pay quite significant dividends of around 6 percent or more.

In addition, the volatility of nontraded REITs has historically been estimated at about half that of traded REITS or the stock market.

Direct real estate ownership also offers investors inflation protection. If you owned a house in the 1970s, you probably experienced a substantial increase in your home's value as a result of inflation. Nearly any type of tangible asset increases in value with inflation. Replacement costs increase, wages rise, and owners charge higher rents.

Determining the performance of nontraded REITs can be a bit tricky because the category is relatively new and data are not widely available. Furthermore, because funds are raised over years rather than on a single day, it can be very difficult to calculate performance exactly, and individual investors' experience can vary dramatically.

Still, as the industry has become quite established, more data and associated estimates are becoming available. A recent study that analyzed nontraded REITs that had gone full cycle (returned investors' funds through either cash payment or becoming a listed security) between 1990 and 2011 calculated average annual returns of 10.3 percent per year and a median return of 10.85 percent.[6]

These performance numbers trailed the average return of the National Council of Real Estate Investment Fiduciaries (NCREIF) Property Index representing institutional investors by only 1.4 percent per year. Given that the NCREIF index represents only voluntarily reported returns of large, sophisticated institutions and that the index ignores all fees, net returns earned by individual investors in nontraded REITs look remarkably strong.

Moreover, there is no straightforward or even approximate means of copying the performance of the NCREIF index, unlike the S&P 500, which can be easily replicated by individuals. In addition, the nontraded REITs' returns are realized individual investor returns. The difference between these returns and the returns voluntarily reported by institutions is minimal, unlike the vast performance shortfall that individual investors often earn in the stock market.

On the downside, nontraded REITs require commitment. Unlike stocks, you can't buy them today and sell them tomorrow. This can be unattractive for many people, although I believe it actually works in investors' favor much of the time because it removes the ability to panic. Once you make the investment, you are likely to be in it for several years. While many programs offer an out after some time period, when you buy a nontraded REIT, you really need to assume that you will hold the investment for several years. You are at the mercy of the management you have entrusted your funds to. It will eventually determine the best time to either sell the entire company to another firm or list the company's stock, providing you with the opportunity to sell your holding. This usually happens around five to seven years after the original investment, although some nontraded REITs have completed this cycle in as little as nine months or taken as long as ten years.

Outside of nontraded REITs, other means also exist to target direct real estate investment. Smaller investments through limited partnerships that pool much less money—think millions rather than billions—are available, but they usually target a much smaller opportunity while also carrying more risk, often because of a narrower or more aggressive focus.

Unlike stocks, nontraded REITs are currently available only through financial professionals, so you have to work with someone to invest in one.

Fortunately for investors, the direct real estate industry is continually changing and improving. High investor interest has encouraged much greater competition across offerings while also resulting in more possibilities. Fees have been driven down, and investment managers are experimenting with structures that offer greater liquidity, including designs that may offer complete liquidity similar to that of stocks. While some of these structures may lose some of the benefits of traditional direct real estate investments, the evolution of the category should continue to offer investors greater choice and higher-quality offerings.

Looking forward, this sector is likely to remain a large and valuable investment category for both endowments and individual investors. Today, I believe nontraded REITs offer individual investors the best means to invest directly in high-quality commercial real estate. But the future may bring new and better options that preserve direct real estate's performance expectations of strong returns, high yields, and inflation protection along with limited correlation with other assets and much lower volatility.

## Private Equity

By definition, private equity describes investments in a private company's stock. Defined this way, private equity doesn't seem too different from an investment in the stock market. In some ways this is true, but just as direct real estate investments perform dramatically differently from publicly traded REITs, direct investments in private companies perform very differently from publicly traded stocks.

While private equity includes any investment in private companies, most endowments target only firms that are already profitable and have a proven concept or business plan. Owners may need more capital to exploit growth opportunities, or they may simply want out of the business.

Return targets for the category remain consistently high. Harvard's 20-year returns ending June 2011 exceeded 20 percent per year,[7] while Yale's returns from 1973 to 2010 reached an astonishing 30.3 percent per year.[8] Individual investors should probably never plan on hitting numbers close to Yale's, but endowments' use of this asset class is easy to understand.

Private equity funds often serve as a bridge for smaller firms, helping them achieve much greater size and scale. The firms they invest in may eventually go public, or the investors may just grow the company to a particular size and sell it to a new owner, such as a larger firm or even another private equity firm.

While private equity is a common component of endowment portfolios, endowments rarely engage in a related investment, venture capital, which targets very small companies in the concept stage of development. The risk is too high. These firms lack a proven concept and may not even have developed to the point of generating any revenue.

Firms at the concept stage may become the next Apple or Google, but the risk of unproven concepts makes the probability of losses dramatically higher. Venture capital investors specialize in high-risk, high-reward investments, and they assume that the majority of their deals will fail. The plan is that one big success will more than compensate for the other failures, but if that outstanding success fails to materialize, returns can be dismal.

Like endowments, individual investors are usually much better served by private equity investments than by venture capital. The category certainly carries risk, but success in helping already successful companies continue to grow is far more likely than finding the next Google or Facebook.

Finding replicas of endowment-model investments in the private equity sector can be more difficult for individual investors. Your approach may also be affected by the amount of funds you have because some investments are available only to people who meet certain net worth or income requirements.

If you have a million-dollar net worth excluding the value of your primary residence, or if your income is above $200,000 for an individual or $300,000 for a couple, the investment industry considers you an accredited investor. Investors meeting these criteria gain access to a much broader array of investments because they are considered to have greater sophistication regarding investments, either because they are more knowledgeable themselves or because they can afford to hire experts on their behalf. Accredited investor status also removes a bit of the protection offered smaller investors.

In the private equity sector, many investments in past years have been available only to accredited investors and have often required fairly high minimum investments. Many of the offerings have also closely resembled the investment structures used by endowments. This may sound good, since we are trying to emulate much that endowments do, but more complex structures tended to limit many investors' access to private equity.

Minimum investments are often as much as $200,000 for an investment with an expected life span of 10 years. Few investors have the financial resources to build a well-diversified portfolio with blocks of this size. The private equity fund may contain excellent diversification, but if your portfolio must stretch to include one fund, it will suffer from lack of diversification across funds and an inflexible design that will see large chunks of your funds become liquid at very infrequent intervals.

Fortunately, increased interest in alternative investments is driving development in this sector as well. As investment managers seek to raise funds from more sources, designs are becoming more flexible, including shrinking minimum investments and shortened time frames. The trend should continue, given the rapidly expanding interest in the sector.

Investment providers also recognize that many investors would like to add this category to their portfolios, but do not meet the accredited investor standards. Investment firms recognize the potential of this market. To date, few offerings exist for nonaccredited investors, but I know that several firms have projects underway.

Over the last few years, however, a modified version of private equity has become widely available to smaller investors through the use of a structure called a business development company (BDC). The 2007–2009 economic and financial meltdown changed the banking and debt industry dramatically. Even years later, firms that may have enjoyed easy and relatively low-cost debt financing are struggling to access credit markets.

Several of the world's largest private equity firms recognized a major hole in the market and stepped in to fill a need. Private equity firms almost always employ large amounts of debt in their deal structures. If they buy a firm for $80 million, they may finance 80 percent or even more of the purchase through debt. Given their high level of sophistication in debt markets, it's not surprising they have led with the development of a hybrid structure that employs both debt and equity.

This modified offering differs from more traditional private equity in several ways. Investors supply funds to a manager who loans the funds to private companies. As part of the deal terms, the manager also secures some type of equity participation in the new company. As a lender, the investor benefits from interest payments from the fund that often exceed 6 percent, and he can also earn returns from the associated equity holdings. As the company grows, the equity holdings can increase in value just as they would in a traditional private equity investment. Some of the structures may also add to returns through increasing loan values, especially if the offering includes loans that are in distress.

Because investors hold the debt on the companies, they enjoy higher priority in the firms' capital structure. If a problem arises, debt holders get paid before equity holders. As a result, investors in debt assume less risk than equity investors. Since the investment combines debt and higher-risk equity, return targets fall below those of pure private equity. In exchange, risk levels should also be less.

Most firms target total returns ranging from the mid-teens to high single digits.

Private equity as a category has a relatively low correlation with most other asset classes, although some correlation with the stock market obviously exists, since one of the potential exits for investors is going public on the stock market.

Long-term data on the hybrid debt and equity structure don't exist, since the first such investment was introduced in 2009. The inclusion of debt in the design and the resulting decrease in dependence on equity returns should lessen correlation with the stock market and probably almost every other investment.

If income is important, the high yield of the investment can be attractive. In addition, many of the offerings provide liquidity on a quarterly basis, although this provision can be shut off either by the board of directors or because there are too many requests for redemptions.

## Real Assets

In addition to real estate, most endowments include a fairly significant allocation to various real assets in their portfolios. Real assets include oil and gas, commodities, timber, precious metals such as gold, and many other tangible assets. Endowments like these assets because they frequently offer solid returns, limited correlation with other investments, and a high level of inflation protection.

As with all other alternative investments, new opportunities continue to expand individual investors' access to this asset class. The two real assets that are most accessible to individuals probably remain oil and gas and traded commodities.

### Oil and Gas

Fossil fuels provide nearly all the energy used in the United States, and despite the growth of various green energy sources, oil and gas will likely remain the main sources of energy in the United States for decades. The recent surge in the availability of natural gas highlights the United States' massive reserves of a much cleaner-burning fossil fuel. By itself, the rapid expansion of natural gas availability in the United States should have tremendously positive effects across the United States and even for the global economy. And investors have ample means to participate in the growth of this sector. Many, if not most, oil and gas investments also offer tax benefits that can make any investment significantly more attractive.

Partly to secure the tax benefits, most of these investments are structured as limited partnerships. This structure also secures many of the other benefits that are desirable in a direct investment, such as insulation from public markets.

Oil and gas offerings vary tremendously across multiple different dimensions and can differ in terms of energy type, geographical focus, tax emphasis, source of profits, and other characteristics. An investment may focus on drilling, creating a land bank for future sale, or generating royalties for investors. The possibilities are many and growing.

Many offerings focus on generating high levels of income and can act as a great addition to a portfolio seeking income. As with many of the other sectors, the lack of correlation with other assets along with the higher return potential can be attractive.

Historically, nearly all oil and gas programs have been available only to accredited investors. This is starting to change with the introduction of new investment structures, although the vast majority of programs still require accredited investor status.

Like nontraded REITs and most private equity, most oil and gas offerings must be purchased through a financial professional, making their inclusion challenging for dedicated do-it-yourselfers. Greater demand for these investments should result in continued evolution of this sector, just like the others already covered.

## Commodities

Endowments like other forms of commodities as well. The means they use to invest in these commodities can be difficult for individuals to duplicate, unlike oil and gas. When building a commodities portfolio, many large institutions use futures contracts to implement complex investment strategies. This is beyond the reach of most individuals, and even much larger investment structures such as mutual funds that employ these approaches often struggle to provide investors with returns that approach the underlying returns of the commodities themselves. The difficulty of storing commodities other than gold, and possibly a few other precious metals, makes physical ownership as a strategy nearly impossible. What do you do with a full oil tanker?

If an individual wants to add commodities to a portfolio, one of the easiest means of doing so remains buying the stocks of companies operating in various natural resource sectors, such as metals, agriculture, and energy. This investment strategy, known as a pure play, enables investors to secure exposure to different commodities while also benefiting from the company management's ability to enhance returns.

This approach can work well, but it has inherent limitations. Company management may not add value or may not add as much as investors hoped, and correlation with the underlying commodities may be weak, particularly in the short term. As mentioned earlier with traded REITs, it's highly likely that stock market movements will heavily influence returns and volatility, although more exact pricing on commodities lessens this trend somewhat. This approach can work as a substitute for difficult-to-achieve direct commodity investments, and it can provide an efficient means to secure exposure to this sector.

A caution may be needed here. Commodities can be volatile, and many people struggle to understand their behavior, given its lack of correlation with so many other commonly held assets. Successful investing in commodities can also be highly dependent on the exact strategy chosen. If you move forward with this asset class, make sure you are highly confident that your strategy fits your needs.

A commodities investment through individual company stocks may be best undertaken with the help of a financial professional, but it doesn't require one. Since the holdings are just individual stocks, anyone can build their own portfolio, leaving this option open to implementation without help.

## Absolute Return

Nearly all endowments include some version of this category, and so it might seem that I would unequivocally advocate adding these investments to an individual investor's portfolio like the previous asset classes covered. This can be true for some investments, but the category as a whole requires considerable skepticism. Returns quoted can be highly misleading, and, as a category, access to investments offering the best returns can be difficult for individual investors.

The term *absolute return* refers to investments in traded securities such as stocks and bonds that have reduced or limited correlation with the stock and bond markets. The name can cause confusion even among financial professionals because it implies that returns will always be positive, or absolute. A better name would have been *independent return*, but this is now such an established category that the name seems unlikely to evolve.

### Managed Futures

These investments make up a much smaller part of the absolute return investments category than some others, but I'm covering them first because they are much more accessible to individual investors. *Managed futures* describes an investment fund managed by a professional that trades in futures contracts. Futures contracts are standardized agreements to buy or sell a particular type and quantity of an asset at an agreed-upon price for future delivery. Individuals may use futures contracts to buy wine today that is still in the barrel and will be delivered after it is bottled. Futures contracts exist for nearly every type of asset, including stocks, bonds, currencies, and commodities.

As an investment category, managed futures usually seek to identify trends in the pricing of an asset and then profitably buy and sell futures contracts to benefit from pricing changes. The investment approach usually depends heavily on computer-driven models, often referred to as black boxes, that identify profit opportunities.

Through managed futures, individual investors can add an asset class that has performed well over time and has low correlation with most other assets. Possibly as important, managed futures often perform well when equities fall. For example, in 2008, many very strong trends—mostly negative—helped managed futures managers post excellent returns while the stock market fell 37 percent.

Overall, many of the offerings available to individual investors consistently offer high quality, and returns for individual investors usually don't differ too much from those on institutional offerings. Many strategies are also available to individuals, although accredited investors have more choices. Notably, the industry has a fairly long history, unlike many other alternative investments.

Yet managed futures can also present challenges. For the category as a whole, returns are usually fairly volatile. Possibly more difficult for most investors, returns are generated by a mysterious black box, and the cause of gains or losses can rarely be clearly explained.

Hence, the investment offers the potential of a good-performing asset and increased portfolio diversification, but its volatility and its mysterious performance may override the benefits for investors who are prone to nervousness. Success or failure that's difficult to understand or explain can be understandably frustrating for many people.

Like most of the alternative investments discussed previously, managed futures are usually available only through a financial professional. Yet even financial professionals will rarely be able to explain the reasons for the performance of a particular offering given their secretive trading strategies. More likely, they will advise for or against particular offerings based on past performance and the reputation of the firm or particular management.

## Hedge Funds

Endowments often include managed futures in their allocations, but hedge funds usually receive larger allocations. Yet for most individuals, following a similar practice probably doesn't make sense because high-quality offerings that are available to individual investors can be difficult to find.

Hedge funds describe investments that seek to limit or even eliminate the impact of stock market movements on a particular trading strategy. To do so, managers hedge away some or all of the market risk. Hedge fund managers' common use of hedging strategies to limit market risk results in their name.

Hedge fund strategies vary tremendously, and approximately 10 distinct types of investment styles exist. While no one strategy can describe all the different categories, some themes exist across several of them. Most approaches attempt to profit from predictable price movements of specific stocks that will be independent of the movements of the stock market.

For example, when companies begin a merger, investors may determine that the prices of the two stocks are inconsistent with their underlying values. Analysts may believe that one company is overvalued by 10 percent, while the other is undervalued by 30 percent. If the analysts' valuation assessments are accurate, there is an opportunity to profit as the stocks move toward their projected fair values. The prices don't need to move to the exact values projected in order to generate profits. Rather, as long as prices move in a direction that lessens price discrepancies, the right strategy will generate a profit.

A hedge fund can short the overvalued company's stock and buy the undervalued company's stock, with the expectation that the stocks will move to their respective fair values. When a stock is shorted, it is borrowed from a third party and sold, with the intention of buying it back later at a lower price. If the two stocks move toward valuations that are closer to their projected fair values, investors using such a strategy will earn a profit regardless of the direction in which the market moves. Profits are driven solely by the relative price movements of the two stocks. Exposure to the market has been hedged away through creating a trading strategy that is dependent on the relative price movements of two stocks rather than on the gains or losses of the general market.

This strategy and various other hedge fund strategies can appear foolproof. Yet success is never certain. Even the best analysis can be derailed by random events or by the fallibility of human analysis. In the previous example, a seemingly surefire assumption that one company is undervalued could be upset by accounting errors or by a natural disaster like the Japanese earthquake of 2011. And, the analysts' projections could simply be wrong, or the market may fail to recognize pricing discrepancies in the near term, forcing a sale before profits are realized.

Still, overall, hedge funds have generated a lot of interest, resulting in rapid growth. In 1990, 530 hedge funds managed around $50 billion in assets. By the end of 2009, more than 8,000 hedge funds held assets of over $1.6 trillion.[9]

This growth results from investors' common desire for solid returns with limited market correlation. Institutions, including endowments, drove the original growth, and high-net-worth individuals are increasingly including this category. But many people, including me, argue that the potential benefits of hedge funds are often overstated.

A very thorough and fairly recent study of hedge funds provides some insight into the benefits and challenges offered by hedge funds. The study analyzed 13,383 funds used by institutions from January 1995 to December 2009. Overall, the authors were fairly complimentary of the hedge fund industry, noting the relatively small number of down years and limited losses. Overall returns appeared fairly strong at 14.88 percent per year net of fees. The strong return numbers explain much of the growing interest.

But correcting for various biases, such as survivorship bias, which commonly plagues mutual funds, and a new one, backfill bias, reduced annual returns all the way down to 7.7 percent.[10] By comparison, the S&P500 returned 7.9 percent per year over the same time period. Backfill bias results when new, successful funds add their historical performance numbers to various databases after they become large enough for inclusion in those databases. Their historical returns tend to cause an upward bias in the overall return data because only favorable early returns are typically reported, and, of course, only successful funds are ever added to the database, since the failed funds disappear.

Even after the adjustment, historical returns remain somewhat attractive, particularly when their diversification potential is included. The authors concluded that 3.00 percent of the returns resulted from activities that were unrelated to market returns, leaving only 4.70 percent resulting from market movement. Hedge funds may not completely remove the market's influence, but they often reduce it significantly.

In spite of their potential value, investments in this category should be approached warily by individual investors. The numbers just given represent returns of institutions with large amounts of capital. Their size and due diligence resources provide them with access to high-quality managers on favorable terms. Unfortunately, the hedge fund category still presents more barriers to entry for individual investors than almost any other asset class. This is changing as more programs target individual investors, but progress remains slow. Many of the best managers using the most successful strategies work only with their established partners, who usually bring to the table hundreds of millions to invest.

Individual investors often are left with the cast-off managers who could not make it in the big leagues or have not proven their abilities. For instance, in this study, the authors noted that the smaller half of the funds earned returns of 6.85 percent per year, trailing the category average by 0.85 percent.[11] And these numbers still represent funds that were large enough to target institutions. Even though institutions like the category, I believe that these investments, more than any other category, require a cautious approach.

Like many other investments, most offerings are available only through a financial professional. The knowledge and experience of your financial professional will probably influence your decision on whether to include or exclude this type of investment.

If you decide to include the category, your choice of investments can be somewhat complicated because of the diverse subcategories and even specific strategies within them. Some investors instead choose to go with a fund-of-funds approach that combines multiple categories into one investment. The primary advantages of this approach are diversification and due diligence by another manager. The disadvantage is very simple—another layer of fees, as the creator of the funds-of-funds offering usually adds another cost to the investment. This would obviously be another area you would want to discuss with your financial professional if you choose to add this investment.

## Performance-Oriented Assets

Up to this point, we have covered the primary asset classes that an endowment would use to generate performance in its portfolio. These investments all target high returns and low, or at least reduced, cross-correlation. The strategy is not complex, as the primary categories include only U.S. stocks; foreign developed market stocks; emerging market stocks; real assets such as real estate, oil and gas, and traded commodities; private equity, including hybrid debt offerings; and absolute return vehicles, which for individual investors will usually mean managed futures.

After diversifying their performance-oriented assets, endowments usually have much more confidence that this part of their portfolio will perform more consistently. As a result, they usually increase its percentage of their portfolios at the expense of the assumed more conservative category of fixed income. Yet, just because they reduce their fixed-income holdings doesn't mean that they ignore the category.

## Fixed Income

Although the major changes in endowments' portfolios remain altering the composition of the performance side of the portfolio and then enlarging it, they haven't left the remaining fixed-income portion completely unchanged. Given that investors somehow managed to underperform bonds by an even greater degree than stocks, incorporating some of the practices of endowments in this area seems wise.

## International and Inflation-Protected Bonds

Just like individual investors, endowments seek various means of defraying the obvious impact of ultra-low interest rates. Approaches differ, but a common thread usually centers on diversifying away from standard U.S. government bonds by adding various other instruments that may earn higher yields or benefit from inflation. This can include investments in foreign fixed-income instruments paying higher interest rates or various types of inflation-protected bonds. These investments can offer higher returns, and the risks will differ, which adds diversification.

Investing in foreign bonds via ETFs has grown dramatically easier over the past few years, and the trend is likely to continue, providing investors with much greater access to developed and emerging foreign debt markets. Of course, just because you can invest internationally doesn't mean that you should. But the increased return and diversification opportunities provide individuals with many ways to improve the expected returns on this part of a portfolio.

Yet, expectations should probably remain restrained. Even though many foreign debt markets probably offer better returns for their given level of risk, interest rates worldwide remain historically low. Many opportunities exist overseas because investors haven't fully embraced international markets. Risk differs from that in U.S. markets, and holdings in different currencies also expose investors to currency risk.

Investors who are comfortable with international fixed income may want to move about a third of their fixed-income holdings into foreign bonds, as many endowments have done. The same percentages can apply to some version of inflation-protected bonds. Many endowments follow a similar approach.

## High-Yield Bonds

Another means of diversifying fixed-income holdings can include high-yield bonds. High-yield, or junk, bonds pay investors significantly higher interest rates to compensate them for the greater risk of default. Unlike investment-grade bond yields, which are tied closely to current government bond rates or Federal Reserve rates, junk-bond yields are more closely correlated with the underlying health of the parent company, the way a stock is, since various problems that the company could face will affect its ability to pay bondholders and return the loan principal. Current interest rates affect their value, but remain much less important unless the bond ratings improve to investment grade, which can happen if the company's financial health improves significantly.

Not surprisingly, during times of distress, junk bonds tend to decline in value the way stocks do because the risk of default increases. By contrast, investment-grade bonds, particularly government bonds, increase in value at such times, as investors flee to safety.

Junk bonds can also present investors with a few other challenges, as their risk/reward profiles can be inconsistent and unpredictable over time. The high-yield category isn't bad, but it can be complex, requiring more expertise than many individuals, and even professionals, have or want to develop. As a result, many investors may want to avoid the category, or add it only if they or their financial advisor have strong experience with or interest in the investment.

Many endowments avoid the category entirely, while others include it, but may count it as a performance asset given its return and risk profile, even though it will nearly always be categorized as fixed income.

When developing your strategy for your fixed-income investments, a key component of your goal should be limiting the risk of the entire asset class through a prudent approach. Bonds should be a safe haven. They hold funds that provide some income and reserves that can be tapped if everything else struggles. Diversifying into international or inflation-protection bonds can make sense, but don't make these changes in an attempt to increase your returns dramatically. This part of your portfolio should protect your wealth from significant loss while providing a bit of return that might even keep pace with inflation. The enhancements just mentioned can help, but they will not turn your fixed-income investments into high performers. That is not their purpose.

The dismal past performance of so many individual investors in fixed income highlights their mismanagement of the category. Too many investors have jumped to the safety of fixed income after stock prices have declined and bond prices have jumped, and then stayed in the bonds too long, getting out only after the bonds have declined and stocks have jumped. If you don't understand an approach, sector, category, international market, or whatever, don't bother. It's not worth it. This applies doubly to high-yield bonds.

Finally, as with U.S. stock investments, many means to invest in fixed income are available to the do-it-yourself investor. Bond ETFs and mutual funds are common, and ETFs in particular have multiplied dramatically over the past several years. As with all the other sectors, financial professionals can offer value in this category, too, but unlike with many investments, you can easily choose to go it alone if you desire. If you choose to manage your own fixed-income holdings, be sure your expected benefits outweigh the risk of forsaking professional assistance, since individual investors' track records suggest that most people lack basic proficiency with an asset that can appear deceptively simpler than it is.

## Fixed-Income Alternatives

The fixed-income category title obviously suggests that bonds of one type or another fill this asset class. This is true for most endowments and institutions. But, just as financial markets continue to create numerous new opportunities in more risk-oriented investments, new offerings targeting safer investments continue to evolve as well. Many of these are targeted toward the needs of individual investors.

Probably the biggest growth area over the past decade plus has been in structured products, or the insurance industry's version, fixed-indexed annuities. These financial instruments generally seek to provide a downside guarantee for your funds combined with upside participation linked to higher-risk assets, such as the stock market or a commodities index. If the market goes down, assets are protected from loss, but if it goes up, the value of the account increases.

There is a catch. On the upside, gains will be capped or prorated in some way. Over time, the account will not earn all the upside without exposure to any of the downside.

The attractiveness of having a potential upside with no downside risk has helped this sector grow considerably since the late 1990s. The growth and size of the industry has also encouraged considerable competition among providers, resulting in constant evolution of products.

The pluses for most of these offerings are usually pretty easy to understand. They offer various assurances against loss; for the insurance products the states back up the insurance company's collateral. Insurance company offerings in the form of annuities can also enjoy significant tax benefits.

The downside in nearly all cases will be decreased flexibility, as investors must commit funds for time spans that can last up to and even beyond a decade. These products can also be confusing, as they often have many moving parts that can act somewhat differently from what the investor expected. For instance, even during the tremendous stock market recovery of 2009 and 2010, many of these products failed to participate in any gains because the high volatility of the markets triggered internal product mechanisms that negated market increases.

Performance that differs from that of other asset classes can make these products attractive, as their returns normally differ from those of nearly any other type of investment. But their peculiarities can carry a downside. The unexpected strength of bond markets through 2011 left some holders of structured products and fixed-indexed annuities wishing that they had left their more conservative investments in bonds rather than putting them in these more complex products. As with nearly any investment, these products can deliver value to a portfolio, but careful consideration before proceeding always makes sense.

# 7

# Self-Management Opportunity

THE PREVIOUS CHAPTERS OUTLINED AN INVESTMENT STRATEGY
that incorporates multiple asset classes into a diversified portfolio
that seeks to leverage the strengths of various investments while minimizing their weaknesses. The success of high-profile endowments
and institutions using this approach has resulted in much study of
the strategy and wide adoption of similar approaches across nearly
the entire institutional investment community, including very high-
net-worth investors.

Yet for some people, the reduction of emphasis on U.S. stocks and
the exclusion of strategies that target market outperformance may
seem limiting, or even foolish. After all, it seems that there must
be some validity behind all the subscription newsletters and other
sources offering hot stock tips. Hopefully, the TV shows and news-
letter industry offer something of value besides entertainment.

Well, in short, a different approach can yield success. The bigger
questions can be what to do with these strategies and how to use them
successfully to make portfolio and retirement success more likely.

I am going to present one stock management approach that is
fairly well known and documented as a proxy for the many different

possibilities available to individual investors. After covering how it works and what it can offer, we will explore some of its possible uses as well as the likely challenges it presents.

## Dow Dividend Strategy

This popular stock management system can offer individual investors several benefits. It's easy to understand and implement, and it has produced strong average annual performance over a long time period. From 1973 through 2011,[1] returns averaged 12.7 percent per year for the standard strategy and 14.4 percent per year for the more aggressive version. This compares favorably to the S&P 500, which returned 9.6 percent per year over the same time period.

Over the more recent lost decade of 2000–2011, the Dow Dividend Strategy outperformed again, returning 3.9 percent per year while the more aggressive strategy provided 4.2 percent gains annually. These numbers weren't great, but they handily beat the S&P 500's annual 0.55 percent returns over the same 12-year period.

In addition, some of the additional return results from higher dividend yields, which can be attractive if you need your portfolio to generate income. While stock prices move considerably, dividend yields tend to be much steadier, with a strong upward bias over time.

Keep in mind that none of these numbers include trading costs or tax impacts. Also, for calculation purposes, the allocations across all stocks were assumed to be exact dollar amounts, and all stock transactions were assumed to occur at the closing prices on the last day of the year. In other words, no investor got exactly these numbers, although someone who was following the system should have come very close.

## How It Works

In this system, only the 30 stocks that make up the Dow Jones Industrial Average, or the "Dow" for short, are considered as potential buys and sells. The Dow is made up of 30 stocks that represent different economic sectors. The combination of all the stocks into one index was created as a representation of the U.S. economy.

In order for these companies to be leaders in their industries, they must be among the most dominant companies in the world. They have tremendous market depth and strength, and they have consistently performed at an exceptional level. If a company doesn't maintain a high performance level, it will cease to be a market leader and will ultimately be removed from the index and replaced by a company that better represents the best of that industry.

A key component of the Dow Dividend Strategy is purchasing only the stocks of companies that are in the Dow. By limiting your purchases to these companies, you've automatically selected from among the best of the best.

First, the system narrows the potential purchase pool to the stocks in the Dow Jones Industrial Average. Next, which stocks are purchased is based on their dividend rate. The dividend rate is the dividend paid per share divided by the share price. The resulting fraction can be converted into a dividend yield percentage by multiplying by 100. Note that the website Dogs of the Dow (www.dogsofthedow.com) does all this, including ranking stocks in the order of highest to lowest dividend rate. In other words, this is really simple because it requires no actual work other than going to the website. After the dividend rates have been determined, the 10 stocks with the highest dividend rates are selected for eventual purchase.

Before the stocks are purchased, the dollar amount that will be invested in each individual stock must be determined by dividing the total amount that will be invested in the strategy by 10. This provides an approximate dollar amount to invest in each of the 10 stocks.

Once the dollar amount to invest in each stock is known, the planned investment amount is divided by the actual share price to determine how many shares of each stock to purchase. Generally, the number of shares that will be purchased must be rounded down to the nearest whole number if you are to have enough funds to buy all 10 stocks. Most firms don't allow purchases of fractional shares, and rounding up may result in purchases that cost more than you have to invest. It's nearly impossible to hold the same dollar amount of each stock because the shares prices simply won't cooperate. The goal is to hold roughly equal dollar amounts of each position.

For smaller portfolios, that is, portfolios under $20,000, executing this strategy becomes a bit more challenging, but it is still doable. Finding a discount brokerage firm with low trading fees is also helpful in keeping trading costs as a percentage of the portfolio to a minimum.

Another historical tendency can help with decisions. The stocks with the lower share prices, the top five, tend to outperform their cousins with higher share prices. Since some holdings will be greater than others, it makes sense to round up the number of shares to purchase for the stocks with the lowest share prices, and then round down the number of shares to purchase for the more expensive stocks.

After this first step has been completed, the portfolio will hold approximately equal investments in 10 different Dow Jones Industrial Average stocks. The performance numbers for the Dow Dividend Strategy cited at the beginning of the chapter assume that all purchases and sales are completed at the closing price on the last trading day of the year. While no investor can realistically achieve this, the assumption assures repeatable and measurable data.

Then, the system does nothing for the next 12 months. That's right, nothing—or at least, nothing with the stocks in this system. At the end of 12 months, the process is repeated to ensure that approximately equal amounts of the 10 stocks with the highest dividend yields in the Dow index are held. If a stock is removed from the Dow index, it is automatically sold and replaced.

As stock prices and dividends fluctuate from year to year, some stocks will be sold because they no longer meet the holding criteria, and new positions will be added. Some positions will also need to be adjusted to bring them back into balance with the other holdings. If a stock has increased in value, but it still makes the dividend yield list, some shares of this winner will need to be sold to bring its allocation back in line. Similarly, if a position has lost value, a purchase of additional shares may be required to bring the allocation back up.

Common sense in rebalancing the portfolio is needed because the ultimate aim is making money, not building a mathematically perfect allocation. If one of the holdings is marginally smaller than the other positions, there's no reason to make the trade. Paying $15 in fees to make a $150 trade incurs a disproportionate cost. This cost will more than offset any benefit gained from achieving near perfection.

Trading efficiency however, should never become an excuse for allowing a portfolio to become unbalanced. Good management should limit percentage differences between stocks immediately after rebalancing. For portfolios in excess of $100,000, holdings should be within a small fraction of a percentage point of each other after rebalancing.

That really is the whole system. The more aggressive version makes a slight change. Out of the 10 original stocks with the highest dividend yield, purchase and manage the 5 stocks with the lowest stock price, not the highest dividend yield, according to the same system. That's the only difference—5 stocks versus 10. Of course, because this version of the system uses only 5 stocks, risk is higher, since 20 percent of the stock portfolio is allocated to each stock. Moreover, some of these stocks could fall into the same industry sector, adding further concentration to the portfolio.

Customized versions of the same system can also be created by building your own basket of stocks to choose from that represent different industries or different company sizes. A customized basket of stocks can include smaller stocks with greater upside potential or only dividend-paying stocks. This could result in a set of stocks that offer more upside potential as well as a more balanced pool of potential stocks. It can be reasonable to assume that choosing from among smaller stocks with greater growth potential may offer greater upside. The major limitation of this strategy tends to be greater temptation to doubt your decisions. For example, using only the Dow stocks demands that you sell a stock when it is jettisoned from the Dow. How do you make this decision with a customized collection of stocks? Nonetheless, this approach can provide another means to build and manage a stock portfolio.

# Challenges

The simplicity of this system and the performance numbers seem to suggest that anyone can get these numbers easily and should obviously want to. But, let's look at this further. In my experience, following the system requires a level of faith and discipline that nearly everyone, including professional investors, lack. Even though the decisions are simple and mechanical, implementation requires purchases of stocks with higher dividend yields, and these are often stocks that are out of favor. These stocks are buys because investors don't like them for some reason. Similarly, the stocks that must be sold are often the current darlings of the market. The dividend yield probably declined because the share price increased, and the stock's recent gains and promising potential make selling it much more difficult.

This system succeeds because of its inflexible discipline. You must buy the ugly stocks and sell the pretty ones. In fact, the system is often referred to as the "Dogs of the Dow." The dogs of the dow website already mentioned provides lots of great background on the system including easily understood data that can be used to implement and manage the system.

Higher dividend yields result for one of two reasons: either an increasing dividend (the numerator) or a decreasing share price (the denominator). While it is possible that firms can land in the top 10 based on dividend yield because of increased dividends, landing there is usually a result of falling share prices driving up the dividend yield.

During a market decline, share prices usually fall a similar amount, so the relative order of the dividend yield ranking will change very little, if at all. Usually, a company's dividend rate increases relative to those of other firms in the Dow index because its share price falls faster than those of other firms as a result of unfavorable news or expectations. Earnings may have fallen, changing technology may threaten established markets, or potential legal problems may present great uncertainty.

Regardless, stock prices nearly always go down relative to those of other stocks because of bad news that is specific to the company.

While these moves may be temporary, they may not be, and even short-term price declines can seem to last forever when you own the stock.

Usually, almost all the companies with the highest dividend yields will present investors with some valid reasons for concern. You may wonder, legitimately, why should I buy a stock that's been going down, and might go down even further? And, if you have been following the system, you may already own the stock, since it could have barely made the list last year, but then a further price decrease drove the price even lower, requiring you to buy more to keep its allocation constant.

For instance, some past purchases included Philip Morris immediately after it lost a lawsuit that some feared could bankrupt the firm. Bank stocks were also common buys during the 2000–2002 meltdown and the more recent financial meltdown. The system required purchasing Citigroup in 2008 on its plunge down to near zero. Kodak was also on the list for years, sometimes rewarding investors for their faith before dishing out severe losses when it was removed from the Dow in 2004.

Several of the stocks may be from the same industry, which could be experiencing challenges. Moreover, some stocks in the Dow, often the sexiest growth stocks, don't pay dividends, so they will never appear as purchase candidates. For years, Microsoft was a stock picker's darling, but it would never have shown up on the list. Only in 2003, after it had fallen out of favor and begun paying a dividend, would it have become eligible for inclusion.

Yet this system works precisely because it forces investors to buy stocks that have declined in price. It is a basic application of buy low and sell high—or hopefully, higher. Most companies and industries go through cycles. Their stock rises because of market or investor sentiment, and then it plateaus for a while. Also, a company's stock can suffer downward trends, which can potentially last for an extended period of time. Price changes can even occur without a significant change in the underlying business. Within the stocks that make up the Dow, you may see Hewlett-Packard's price shoot up and Home

Depot's price plummet because high-technology stocks are in favor, while housing stocks are a popular as the plague.

In addition to the problem of purchasing out-of-favor stocks, leaving a portfolio alone for the next year can also be nearly impossible for many. Most people will be terribly tempted to "fix" the seemingly obvious problems as more bad news comes out or a great opportunity appears. Sometimes investors feel absolutely compelled to act. The hardest part of this system is literally doing nothing for 12 months, yet this is a major key to its success.

After going through a difficult year, many investors find that rebalancing to buy additional shares of positions that have declined for very legitimate reasons is often just too difficult. Finding individual investors who have executed this strategy successfully remains difficult, and this is unlikely to change. This is obviously not because the system is hard or expensive to manage. It's just too difficult emotionally for rational people to follow. It frequently requires actions that make little sense and go against our self-preservation instincts.

## An Illustration

This strategy provides a great example in several areas. As mentioned, as good as the strategy is, people rarely enjoy similar success in spite of its incredible simplicity. The system is not rocket science. In fact, the average five-year-old who can read is probably more likely to enjoy success with this approach than more experienced investors. The five-year-old doesn't know enough to be scared when it seems they should be.

Comparing this system to any of the many other complex or difficult systems offered by countless newsletters and tip services highlights the challenges of trying to manage according to a particular system. This system is easy, yet it still presents potential followers with difficult and often insurmountable challenges. How far short are individuals likely to fall using much more complex approaches? Again, it's not that these approaches can't work.

Beyond implementation, this system introduces another question. Even if you did follow it exactly, how would you integrate it into a larger portfolio? Should it represent your overall U.S. stock allocation, or should it be treated as something more along the lines of a hedge fund strategy that provides returns that are less linked to the market?

The answer isn't obvious. While the system has provided good returns, they differ from the stock market in sometimes helpful and sometimes destructive ways. From 2000 through 2011, the standard deviation of the returns, a common measure of variation from the average return, was slightly lower than that of the market for the Dow 10-stock strategy, but higher for the more aggressive five-small-stock approach, so the overall volatility differed very little.[2]

Differences in performance showed up in other areas. Losses during the 2008 meltdown for both Dow Dividend Strategies were worse than the S&P 500's 37.0 percent loss. The Dow 10-stock strategy lost 38.3 percent, while the 5-small-stock approach dropped a whopping 49.1 percent. Much of the system's success over the decade results from the 2000–2002 outperformance because all the stocks that were held in the Dow strategies over this period were fairly dull dividend-paying stocks. They declined much less than the general market because the Dow and the S&P 500, as well as most investment strategies, included a large exposure to technology-related companies. The only stock in either Dow strategy from 2000 to 2002 that remotely resembled a tech stock was SBC Communications, one of the remaining stodgy "Baby Bell" companies created through the AT&T breakup. After 2002, the next nine years saw the Dow strategies and the S&P 500 earn almost identical total returns.

The underperformance in some years as well as frequently different performance partly explains the reluctance of many financial professionals to use this simple and easily implemented solution. Most financial professionals learn quickly that few investors can tolerate underperformance for very long, and that many of them tend to have short memories regarding past outperformance. After outperforming the market for three years beginning in 2000, the strategy underperformed for the next three. After a great year in 2006, the Dow Dividend Strategy again underperformed from 2007 through 2009. Over time, the strategy has worked very well, but any financial professional who was heavily dependent on this strategy would have seen his business really struggle during the financial downturn.

Returns probably have enough similarity with the U.S. stock market that any assets allocated to this strategy should probably count toward your U.S. stock allocation. If you are a dedicated do-it-yourselfer, this could provide you with an opportunity to stay involved in a significant part of your portfolio. Yet, if your stock allocation now represents only 15 or 20 percent of your total portfolio, are the effort and potential frustration worth it?

Another approach could be to use this strategy as a home-built hedge fund. Losses for both strategies that remained well under 10 percent (7 percent total for the Dow 10 and 5 percent for the Dow 5) during the period 2000–2002 suggest that it could serve this purpose. This compares very well to losses of nearly 40 percent for the S&P 500 over the same time period.

Yet, as mentioned, losses in 2008 of 38.3 percent and 49.1 percent for the Dow 10 and the Dow 5, respectively, dwarf the average hedge fund loss of 16.74 percent.[3] The high potential for the Dow strategy performance to resemble general stock market performance goes against the primary purpose of diversification. In any event, if this becomes a proxy for a hedge fund, most likely the allocation would be limited to 5 or 10 percent of the total portfolio, which brings up the same question mentioned earlier: is it worth the effort?

In analyzing the value of any stock selection system, this should be a primary consideration. How might the strategy fit into your overall portfolio? What is the real goal for the assets invested in the system? Is the investment reasonably expected to improve the expected returns and volatility of the total portfolio? For some investors, the only goal may be entertainment and challenge. If only 5 percent of a portfolio is used, the rewards of playing an active role in managing a portfolio may far outweigh the relatively inconsequential impact on return. As with nearly any investment, realistic expectations are invaluable.

## Decisions

This whole chapter may have either further convinced you that you have no desire to manage a stock portfolio or moved you off the fence away from doing so. It's not easy, even when it appears so simple. Or, it may have helped you understand how you can remain very involved in a part of your portfolio while incorporating best-in-class investments and resources from various other sources.

Hopefully, this chapter has further convinced you of the value of a more widely diversified portfolio. Even though the Dow Dividend Strategy excelled relative to the wider market over the 2000–2011 period, it still managed to generate returns of only about 4 percent per year excluding all costs and trading fees, and it experienced several periods of underperformance, including even bigger losses than the overall market during the 2007–2009 downturn. Actual returns would probably have trailed these numbers, and my real-life experience suggests that most investors would have abandoned the system long before they enjoyed its benefits. The system also serves as an excellent proxy for many other systems that can work, but that may be challenging to implement and difficult to integrate into a larger portfolio.

$$8$$

# Creating a Portfolio

AS YOU CONSIDER MOVING FORWARD, DETERMINING WHERE TO start may seem daunting. We've covered a lot of concepts and possibilities, and figuring out how to apply them all may seem a bit overwhelming. A few basic decisions can help you get started. By now, you hopefully realize the potential of a good design.

This chapter will start with creating a portfolio that generates substantial income, and we'll also adjust it to meet more specific retirement needs. The next chapter will step through some of the opportunities and challenges of managing all your own funds. In some ways, it's easier than ever to manage your own money, given all the online information and resources that are available. Yet, if you choose to go it alone, many alternatives are unavailable to you, and this can make this approach inferior from several perspectives. And, the rapidly expanding world of investment possibilities makes it harder than ever to best represent yourself. It's a bit like acting as your own mechanic. It was relatively easy a few decades ago, but it has become progressively more difficult as cars have gotten more complicated. Investments have followed a similar progression. Regardless, this choice will have a major impact on your portfolio design.

The following chapter will address how you can profitably partner with a financial professional. As the opportunities and challenges in the investment world have multiplied dramatically, the potential value of a financial professional to help you identify and chart the right course has increased. Just as investment opportunities have greatly expanded, so have the types of potential working relationships available. Forty years ago, a stockbroker was about the only type of financial professional that was available to individual investors. Fortunately, those days are long gone. We will cover some of your possibilities and look at the pros and cons offered by different professional relationships.

## Building a Portfolio

Designing a portfolio can be surprisingly easy for most people once they understand some basic information. There are two general decision areas: (1) what do you want your money to do for you, and (2) what tools are you willing to use to accomplish your purpose? Next, we'll lay your willingness to endure possible losses over the top of these choices to modify the design. This last part is probably the most challenging because developing an exact definition of anyone's risk profile is nearly impossible. A few basic questions, however, can make all of this much easier than it may initially appear.

## Acceptable Withdrawal Rates

Before we go too far, it may be helpful to explore some common assumptions regarding how much of your portfolio you can withdraw annually and still expect your funds to last the rest of your life. There is no right answer, only reasonable projections. As you might expect, because of its importance, this question has generated a great deal of research and speculation. Most studies and financial models reach fairly similar conclusions, although there's ample room for adjustment based on personal circumstances and portfolio design. As you may have already guessed, nearly all studies assume that the starting portfolio is composed of 60 percent stocks and 40 percent bonds, or something very close to that. Using this portfolio construction, the historical performance for stocks and bonds is plugged in for 25 year periods with 1926 often used as the starting year because of the availability of data.

The common conclusion based on historical performance of the stocks and bonds over multiple 25-year time spans including wars, recessions, economic booms and so on is that a portfolio has essentially a 100 percent chance of lasting 25 years if the withdrawal rate starts at 4 percent and increases every year by the rate of inflation.

In my experience, it can be easy to read this incorrectly, so I'll restate it. The original withdrawal amount is determined as 4 percent of the total portfolio, and it is this amount, not the percentage of the withdrawal, that is adjusted upward by the inflation rate. The withdrawal amount grows annually by the rate of inflation regardless of the value of the portfolio which will fluctuate with the value of investments.

If you start with $1,000,000, a 4 percent rate puts the original withdrawal amount at $40,000, and this amount is adjusted upward by the inflation rate. In year 2, the withdrawal amount would be $41,200, assuming an inflation rate of 3 percent (3% × $40,000 = $1,200, which is added to $40,000). It can be easy to assume that withdrawals of only 4 percent of the total portfolio are all that is ever allowed, or that some other constraint that wasn't intended must be applied. Logically, if you withdraw only 4 percent of your portfolio, you will never run out of money, since 96 percent of your portfolio will always remain, but this practice will severely and unnecessarily limit your withdrawal rates. This is not the intention. The original 4 percent withdrawal rate must be adjusted for inflation.

Using these assumptions, an investor is not expected to run out of money because the portfolio, assumed as a 60 percent stock and 40 bond portfolio, is projected to experience growth over time that replaces some or all of annual withdrawal amounts that are growing every year with inflation.

You may be thinking that this withdrawal rate is too low, and it may be. Various other studies suggest that an initial rate of 5 percent may be acceptable. And, if you adopt a more sophisticated strategy like those used by endowments, even higher initial percentages are probably sustainable.

One comment that nearly any study will make pertains to market conditions. If you retired in the late 1960s, before the stock market went sideways for nearly 15 years and interest rates rose for almost as long, your portfolio would have struggled, causing your early withdrawals to have a more severe impact on your total portfolio value. These years were used to create the lower bounds for allowed withdrawal rates projected by the studies.

Conversely, if you retired in 1982, at the start of the tremendous bull market for stocks and bonds, almost any initial withdrawal percentage assumed was likely to be conservative because of the tremendous growth of all parts of the 60/40 stock/bond model.

The 4 percent initial withdrawal rate is purposely conservative, since no portfolios starting in any year—including the late 1960s—ran out before 25 years. If you believe that returns for most assets will be at least average, you can be more optimistic. Or, if you believe that your portfolio is likely to perform better than an average 60/40 stock/bond model, as I do, you can adjust the withdrawal rate up. Your management will also affect these numbers.

If you're already in retirement, you can probably adjust the withdrawal rate up too, although many people in their early seventies may still need to plan for 25 years, especially if they are half of a healthy couple.

## Financial Goals

Most people's requirements for their funds include a combination of total return, income, and possibly liquidity or limitations on volatility. This statement sounds very neat and organized, and much of the industry tends to work very hard to help people identify exact numbers, including quantified measures of risk tolerance and growth expectations.

But in my experience, people tend to want their money to grow by as much as is responsible while providing reasonable income without too much risk. And that's about as defined as they can really get their needs.

This is not meant as an insulting statement. Investors are people, not equations or algorithms. We are far more complex than can ever be captured by a short list of risk and return expectations.

Nearly everyone wants to be responsible with his or her money and create a portfolio that throws off much more money than he or she will probably need. Higher potential income and growth provide a safety cushion while satisfying the desire to do the right thing.

I have found it more constructive to put together a portfolio that can satisfy requirements that might represent an individual at some future point. If we can meet future income requirements while putting together a plan that provides reasonable growth with acceptable risk, we have a good start. If some areas don't seem quite right, or if more flexibility is needed, the hypothetical example can be adjusted. Most people seem to find choosing from or modifying various options far easier than defining their perfect direction.

To facilitate a discussion, I'm going to assume that a husband and wife plan to withdraw $50,000 from a $1,000,000 portfolio. I'm also going to assume that they are newly retired and want the portfolio to generate growth if possible, but not at all costs. They are reasonably comfortable with some risk, but have no intention of going back to work if portfolio losses reach "unacceptable" levels. Like most people, they really don't know how severe losses would have to be before they would really panic, but they know that losing nearly 40 percent, like most investors with all their money in the stock market did during the financial meltdown, would be too much. So, they don't want all their money in stocks, but they also don't like bonds because record low rates offer very little return and high risk of at least some loss. If this all seems vague, it's probably because it is. Yet, this scenario is remarkably common. I set the portfolio value to at least $1,000,000 because it will make this investor an accredited investor—and the math is easy!

Notice that I did not include a requirement that the portfolio can never go down, or that it can decline by only a certain amount. This is much more important than it may appear. If you allow a portfolio's value to fluctuate, both up and down, you can include many different assets with strong upside potential that may also experience shorter-term gains and losses. If you place severe constraints on portfolio value changes, the number of available tools shrinks dramatically, and life is somehow never as predictable as a clear mathematical constraint might require.

## Acceptable Tools

After walking through the various asset classes employed by endowments, we have a potential list of investments that could be added to a portfolio. In the list in Figure 8.1, you could even put a checkmark beside any investment that you think you might like to include in your portfolio. Please note that unless you have a portfolio value of well over $1,000,000, it's unlikely that you will want to include every asset class. Even much larger investors may choose to avoid subcategories such as hedge funds. The subcategories in italics represent the choices that should positively contribute to nearly any portfolio, and could be considered automatic choices.

## Designing a Portfolio

Figure 8.2 shows the allocations employed by the big three super-endowments: Yale, Harvard, and Stanford. It may seem familiar because we already gave the same information in Figure 5.1.

As individual investors, we probably won't copy their design exactly, but it can provide a great starting point. You may remember that Yale has enjoyed incredible success with private equity, and this has led it to allocate a much larger percentage of its assets to this asset class than any other endowment I know of. Yale's 34 percent allocation to private equity skews the average in a direction that probably isn't advisable for an individual investor, so in Figure 8.3,

---

**Figure 8.1**   Potential Investments

**Stocks**

____ *U.S. Stocks (1)*

____ *Foreign Developed Market Stocks (2)*

____ *Emerging Market Stocks (3)*

**Real Assets**

____ *Direct Real Estate Investment (probably via non-traded REITs) (4)*

____ Commodities: Oil and Gas

____ Commodities: Traded Stocks

**Private Equity**

____ Private Equity (new structures evolving)

____ *Debt/Private Equity (probably via BDCs) (5)*

**Absolute Return**

____ Managed Futures

____ Hedge Funds

**Fixed Income**

____ *Domestic Bonds (6)*

____ International Bonds (probably through ETFs)

____ High Yield Bonds

____ Fixed Income Substitute (structure products or fixed index annuities)

---

I created another version excluding Yale. Harvard and Stanford's allocations are pretty similar, with all but two categories, commodities and real estate, falling within 3 percent of each other. If commodities and real estate are combined into one category of real assets, the total allocations for both are exactly 23 percent.

If we start with this allocation, we have a beginning template that may not be too far from where an individual investor might want to end up.

**Figure 8.2** Average Target Allocation for Yale, Harvard, and Stanford (July 2011)

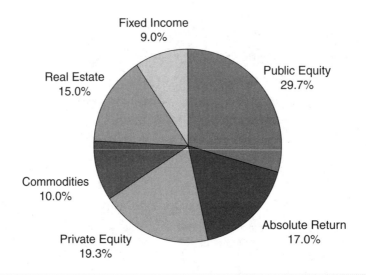

Fixed Income
9.0%

Public Equity
29.7%

Real Estate
15.0%

Commodities
10.0%

Absolute Return
17.0%

Private Equity
19.3%

*Sources:* Yale Endowment Report for 2011; Harvard University Financial Report for 2011; Stanford Management Company Report for 2011.

The asset classes that I listed as automatic inclusions in Figure 8.1 were all public equity, real estate, private equity, and fixed income. If we start with just these, we will need to make some adjustments to the percentages, but we will have a reasonable starting point.

Adjusting the percentages for an individual investor may seem a bit complicated or tedious because investments that are removed must be reallocated elsewhere. But the process is simpler than it looks. Simply reallocate the extra percentages available from assets we eliminated into other categories that seem reasonable.

Since commodities are not included in our allocation, the 10.5 percent allocation made by Harvard and Stanford will need to go elsewhere. The average of real assets for all three endowments was 25 percent, and it dropped to 23 percent without Yale. If we want to avoid over concentrating in real estate, we might drop this allocation to just 20 percent.

**Figure 8.3**    Average Target Allocation for Harvard and Stanford
(July 2011)

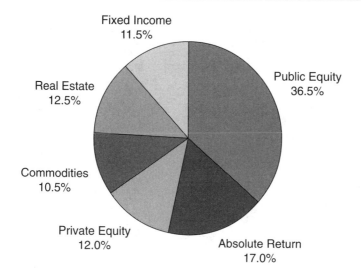

*Sources:* Harvard University Financial Report for 2011; Stanford Management Company Report for 2011.

Similarly, the automatically included asset classes exclude absolute return, so the 17 percent allocated to this area will need to move somewhere else. While the 19 percent average for private equity across all three endowments may be high, we could adjust the 12 percent average allocation of Harvard and Stanford up to an even 15 percent using a small amount of the absolute return. This will leave us with an extra 14 percent unallocated. If we want to keep a more aggressive portfolio, we could move all of this into equities, or we could instead move some of it into fixed income. Adding another 3.5 percent to fixed income moves this category up to 15 percent. We are sacrificing some expected return but adding a bit more of a liquid low-correlation asset class. Our new allocation would look like Figure 8.4. Please note that the public equities are separated into their respective categories for greater clarity.

**Figure 8.4**   Hypothetical Target Allocation

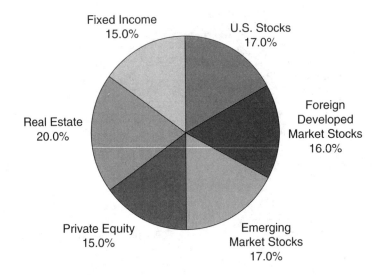

If this process seems less than scientific, it's because it is. Unlike the standard 60/40 portfolio, which is based on widely understood and accepted modern portfolio theory, endowment allocations result from much less exact estimates of future returns and correlations. The availability of stock and bond pricing data that can be used to project future returns and correlations can create the illusion that future performance projections are more exact than they probably are. The lack of exhaustive data for most alternative assets lessens the belief that any particular allocation will definitely be superior to any other. It's a bit like having the choice of several routes to get to a particular destination. At the start, you know the general direction and the choices available, but the best route may not be clear because traffic, construction, stoplights, and accidents can alter the exact results.

The allocation discussed here provides a starting point, not a final solution. We can use it to determine what we like and don't like

**Figure 8.5** Hypothetical Target Allocation Including More Asset Classes

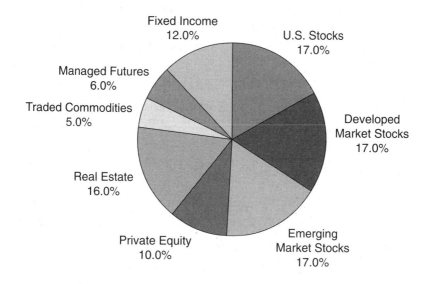

about this design, including income generation and exposure to particular assets. For comparison, Figure 8.5 includes more asset classes and might represent a larger portfolio or the portfolio of an investor who likes more diversification.

Once we have a basic starting portfolio, we can look at some of its characteristics to see where we may want to change it.

Going back to our hypothetical couple who needed $50,000 from a $1,000,000 portfolio, we can use the portfolio in Figure 8.4 to see how this provides for our income. Some assumptions will be required, but they are pretty easy.

## Generating Income

The dividend yield of U.S. stocks during most of 2012 was about 2.0 percent, and foreign market dividends were a bit higher. To provide a bit of padding, a dividend rate of 2.0 percent across all equities will be assumed. Nontraded REITs will be assumed to pay a dividend rate of 6.5 percent, and the private equity will all be placed in hybrid debt/private equity business development companies (BDCs) paying an average dividend rate of 7.0 percent. Lastly, the yield on fixed income will be pegged at 3.5 percent. All these dividend rates can change, and different market conditions may require different assumptions, but they should provide a decent starting point.

Under these assumptions, portfolio income would total $37,750. Using the same assumptions, the total yield of a traditional 60/40 stock/bond model would have been $26,000. Obviously, both of these numbers fall short of the targeted $50,000 needed from the portfolio.

We have a choice: we can cut our income, or we can take the additional funds out of the portfolio by selling some assets. While some investors remain reluctant to ever liquidate an asset, whether return comes through income earned or through capital gains, or whether income is derived from interest or from capital gains, it's all technically return. Capital gains are even preferable from a tax perspective.

The reluctance of many investors to sell assets to generate returns can probably be traced to the characteristics of bonds, which usually have very limited potential for capital gains. If you sell bonds, you are eating into your principal. If you sell stocks, you may be selling only a portion of your gains, and the principal amount may remain larger than your starting value.

The need to sell some holdings to meet income requirements has also become more common because of low rates. When bonds were paying 9 percent, the same 60/40 stock/bond portfolio would have generated income of $48,000 rather than $26,000. Generating income with ultra-low rates requires more imagination than was required during past decades.

In a typical 60/40 portfolio, your choices of what to sell are limited. You can sell either U.S. stocks or U.S. bonds to fund the

$24,000 shortfall. Intelligent management dictates selling whatever has gone up the most or down the least.

In the portfolio with more asset classes, the same practice of selling whatever has gone up the most or down the least still makes sense. But in this case, we need to raise less than half of the cash to fund the $50,000 withdrawal, and we have more choices. Not only do we have three categories of stocks, but the addition of debt/private equity, direct real estate, and international bonds provides more options. In reality, many direct real estate investments offer limited and potentially no liquidity. And, debt/private equity holdings are often liquid, but may return less than the full share price if we liquidate early. So, more stock and bond categories may be the only real addition, which isn't nearly as powerful because their correlations with one another are higher.

Even so, in this example, we need to fund only $12,250 through sales rather than $24,000. Even if our portfolio has dropped in value because of a market or economic slowdown, most and probably all of our income remains, so that we still need only $12,250.

If you depend on your portfolio for income, your portfolio's key attribute isn't necessarily portfolio value. You obviously will care about your total portfolio's worth, since it will ultimately drive your ability to generate income, but it's not the primary issue affecting short-term income generation.

This key realization that endowments made long ago resulted in much of the portfolio design shift we've covered. Just like retirees, endowments need their portfolios to produce income on a regular basis. Yet, the underlying daily portfolio value is much less important. Obviously, they want it to increase over time, but temporary losses don't matter too much as long as an endowment can meet its immediate funding needs through income generation and the sale of assets that have not lost value. Providing that the portfolio design generates income that can be maintained over several years, struggling assets that are hit by temporary challenges will have time to recover.

In the same way, allowing some portfolio flexibility enables you to build a portfolio with strong growth potential and income generation that can also withstand tremendous stress.

In this situation, the $12,250 can come from a number of sources. If stocks are doing well, you can always sell them. This is simple and quick, and most people find it to be pretty easy. But when stocks lose value, especially if it's by more than 10 or 20 percent, most people become understandably nervous. Cash generation from stocks through dividends rarely depends on short-term price movements. Companies don't usually cut dividends, because this action tends to have a severe impact on share prices, which, in turn, affects other issues such as borrowing costs.

If stocks lose value, bond prices usually increase, as enough investors flee into bonds to drive prices up. In our example portfolio with a 15 percent allocation to fixed income, we would have $150,000 in bonds as a backstop. If bonds were sold to fund the shortfall, we would probably be selling an asset that has appreciated a bit, and we would have enough money in bonds to fund approximately 12 years of income at this withdrawal rate.

Since withdrawals would go up over time to fund spending that keeps up with inflation, and since selling the bonds would slightly affect our income generation because the amount invested in bonds would decline, a conservative assumption might project bonds lasting only nine years. During that time, some of the BDCs or non-traded REITs would probably liquidate, providing more opportunities to sell an asset that has hopefully appreciated. And, nine years is extremely pessimistic by any standard. Even during the financial meltdown, the S&P 500 got within 10 percent of its previous highs within about five years. This is not great, but it illustrates that nearly any downturn, including truly horrible economic challenges and correspondingly bad equity markets, has its limits.

In the sample portfolio that includes only 15 percent bonds, equity markets would have to remain exceedingly bad for nearly a decade before the portfolio would be likely to start facing real challenges.

By comparison, a more traditional portfolio suffers more downside exposure, greater volatility, and less upside potential while requiring more sales of fewer assets to generate income. The alternative asset classes would probably provide both greater income and higher total return while smoothing performance.

If we look back at the portfolio with additional assets (Figure 8.5), the advantages of diversification become more apparent, especially in terms of generating income. This portfolio includes an additional two asset classes that are liquid and that historically have experienced limited correlation with most other assets, including stocks. Because these new assets produce less income, the overall projected income would fall to $32,000, but our ability to access managed futures and commodities in addition to the other six asset classes greatly improves the likelihood that income can be generated by selling appreciated assets rather than having to sell a holding that has declined in value.

Moreover, the higher probability that assets other than fixed income could be sold during a downturn adds to the portfolio's flexibility. Fixed income's primary contributions to a portfolio are its low volatility and low correlation with most risk assets. When conditions create challenges for performance assets, which often could result in the sale of bonds to meet income targets, if an asset class other than fixed income can be sold, not only does the portfolio lock in gains on a different asset, but it retains greater flexibility through keeping all of the safer assets, bonds, intact. The safety net remains untouched.

Managed futures in particular have historically performed well during times of distress. If they were included in a portfolio that required the liquidation of assets to fund income needs during a severe market dislocation, it's likely that they would have appreciated in value. By selling them at a profit, not only does the investor realize better returns for the portfolio, but the amounts of the bonds and other diversifying assets in the portfolio remain in place, leaving more flexibility in the portfolio if bad times continue. Better portfolio design can't prevent all losses, but it can dramatically limit the impact of inevitable declines of different investments.

Advanced portfolio design becomes much easier when there is greater clarity regarding the needs for the portfolio. In this case, we wanted income, and we were willing to let the portfolio value fluctuate. A severe market correction might affect U.S. stocks, and because of their higher correlation, many or even all of the foreign stocks might also decline. Yet, the income would probably remain relatively unchanged. Some of the other assets in the portfolio might be adversely affected as well, while others could possibly increase in value.

During 2008, when stocks declined 37 percent, foreign markets generally performed slightly worse than the U.S. market. Some assets, such as managed futures, increased in value, while many other investments, such as real estate, performed much better than equity markets. Yet, for a person depending on his portfolio for income, most dividend payments remained fairly constant. Some stock and real estate dividends were reduced, but total income should have remained relatively unaffected. If our hypothetical couple managed their portfolio reasonably well, bonds and managed futures, if they were in the portfolio, would have provided ample assets that could have been sold at a profit to fund any income shortfall.

Over the next several years, while asset values recovered, the portfolio would have continued to generate most of the income needed, and various assets, particularly bonds, could have been liquidated with gains for income. About four years after the start of the turmoil, some nontraded REITs would have begun liquidating, most of them at a solid profit, providing more income and reinvestment options. In this way, even the incredible economic and market dislocation suffered during the financial crisis could have been managed quite easily using the basic principle of selling only assets that had appreciated.

To be clear, not every holding your portfolio contains will always earn a profit. Judgment is required. During the recent downturn, government and investment-grade bonds as a category performed well. If you held individual bank bonds, however, you probably would not have enjoyed similar success. Similarly, nearly all managed futures programs enjoyed excellent success during 2008. But if your particular managed futures investment somehow suffered a bad year, your choices would have been more limited, and you would have needed to assess the quality of your investment.

Not every stock will increase over time, either. If the value of the equity asset class has increased the most in your portfolio, funding income needs would probably result in selling some stocks. Whatever system you have in place for stock management needs to be followed, which could result in selling stocks at a loss. The greater point is rotating through asset classes and specific assets as the fortunes of various categories rise and fall over time. Greater diversity gives an investor far more choices and demands less dependence on any asset, helping to smooth performance and making panic moves less likely.

## Individual Adjustments

The two sample portfolios in Figures 8.4 and 8.5 represent fairly generic options, yet they can work well for a wide variety of investors. They offer broad diversification, excellent upside potential, high liquidity, and strong income if needed. Yet, these basic models will not fit everyone. Some people may see the higher allocation to bonds as being too conservative, especially with today's low rates and future inflation expectations. Others may feel the opposite and want more of their funds spread across less volatile fixed income or guaranteed assets. Once a starting point is established, modifications can be fairly easy, particularly if you apply a basic checklist.

## Portfolio Checklist

1. *Intellectual.* Does the portfolio design have a high expected probability of success based on history and reasonable expectations of future performance? If the design is similar to that of an endowment, the answer is probably yes.
2. *Emotional.* Can you live with the potential portfolio performance even if various stock markets, real estate markets, other asset classes, or economies struggle, possibly for an extended period of time? A great portfolio design works only if you follow it.

3. *Income if applicable.* Will the portfolio deliver income as needed, including providing various means to supplement investment yields through sales of assets from the portfolio that have not declined in value, even during severe and extended market downturns?

4. *Liquidity.* Are enough of the assets liquid to provide you with ample income and access to funds as needed using reasonable assumptions? Remember that emergencies requiring 40 percent of your portfolio within 30 days are highly unlikely.

5. *Volatility.* Does the portfolio design include enough assets with low enough expected cross-correlation to keep expected volatility low enough for your comfort?

6. Finally, remember that your individual circumstances and desires always trump everything else.

In the list just given, it should be obvious that a well-designed portfolio should have a high probability of success. If you are building a portfolio with a design similar to that used by endowments, this should naturally result.

The other items should also be pretty self-explanatory. The portfolio's ability to keep you emotionally comfortable is worth highlighting, since mismanagement, more often than any other problem, is the primary cause of terrible individual investment performance over time. A better design that increases the likelihood of success should not only increase confidence, but also make the journey easier and more fun.

Usually, investors start their adjustments by determining the percentage of assets invested in performance assets versus those invested more conservatively. The more conservative assets may include bonds or various other investments such as fixed-indexed annuities or structured products. The principle will often remain the same. This part of the portfolio is meant to provide a more stable base, including supplementing income if all or nearly all performance assets struggle.

Going back to the sample portfolios, if the allocation to bonds or other perceived less risky investments is raised from 15 to 30 percent, allocations to more performance-oriented assets can be reduced pro rata across the assets, or specific categories seen as less desirable can be targeted. Similarly, bonds can easily be reduced by moving part of the bond allocation into other categories or adding additional asset classes.

Even if we keep the bond allocation from the original 60/40 stock/bond portfolio, the risk-oriented side of the portfolio can be improved through greater diversification. Diversifying well beyond U.S. stocks seems wise no matter how small the performance part of a portfolio becomes. Any investor should want to maximize performance potential while minimizing risk.

When I work with individual investors, we often create several different portfolios for review and look at the pros and cons of each before deciding on a specific allocation. There is no perfect or right answer. Even the portfolios of endowments and institutions vary considerably, as seen in the earlier comparison of Yale, Harvard, and Stanford.

Optimum allocation decisions will also vary over time. While predicting markets can be difficult, strong trends such as under-valued stock or real estate markets might lead you to increase your allocations to certain sectors a bit.

Of course, you never want to let recent success tempt you into chasing asset classes with overheating prices, such as U.S. stocks in the late 1990s. If anything, overvalued markets should probably act as a warning to back off a bit from some categories. Fortunately, the portfolio's success doesn't depend on timing markets; it just depends on making reasonable decisions. Successfully increasing or decreasing your allocations to markets that are undervalued or over-heated might help your returns a bit, but the model's success results from a predictable and repeatable strategy, not from clairvoyance.

These basic decisions should help you construct a solid portfolio that meets various needs, including income, growth, and protection from loss. No portfolio will ever be perfect, but a good design should tip the odds of success heavily in your favor, both because of expected returns of different asset classes and because of increased ability to manage a portfolio successfully throughout any circumstances.

# 9

# Flying Solo

MOST PEOPLE START OUT MANAGING THEIR OWN MONEY. THEY have to. If you're like me and you had trouble finding two nickels to rub together when you first started out, the concept of having someone help you with your "finances" seemed a bit far-fetched. After all, what could you really do with two nickels?

But after a few years, hopefully your situation changes. You have a bit of excess money, or at least the possibility of some. At this point, most of us develop an approach to "managing" our money. For some, this includes active management and investing, but for many, the approach is more haphazard. Finances are spread across a few bank accounts and financial institutions. As the average person's career moves forward, he may start a retirement plan with one company, then move to a second company and enroll in a second plan. After a few years, assets start to accrue in different places in various accounts. For many people, this constitutes "managing" their money. They work to put a bit aside and feel good that they've got at least some funds available for the future.

And then, for most people, there comes a time when they decide they need to get a bit more serious about investing. Often, life events provide the stimulus for this. A child starting preschool often focuses parents on the eventual need for college tuition. For others, a birthday, a sudden windfall, or impending retirement shines a spotlight on financial issues. When the need is highlighted, most people begin thinking about how best to identify and achieve their goals.

As a result, at some time, nearly every investor begins actively forming and managing toward his or her future investment goals and patterns. As part of their planning, most people make a conscious decision to either manage their money on their own or seek outside help, either from a professional or from a gracious guide, perhaps a relative, who is willing to provide free advice.

By this point, I hope you are convinced of the value of having a solid investment strategy and of the potential pitfalls of following old and tired approaches. Furthermore, I hope that the woeful underperformance of so many investors has convinced you that not everyone is well served by acting as his or her own advisor. If you're unsure of your intentions, the goal of this chapter is to help you decide whether to go it alone or seek outside help. If you decide that flying solo with at least some of your assets makes sense for you, some useful tips should help you achieve greater success, and even if you work with a financial professional on some or all of your portfolio, these practices will be helpful. Regardless of your choice, you will probably be well served by making a specific choice rather than letting inertia guide your future.

## Aptitude, Time, and Desire

In spite of the many dismal performance numbers quoted regarding the success of individual investors, I strongly believe that many people have the potential to manage their own money successfully, particularly in some investment sectors. Increased tools and information along with considerably lower fees all make self-management of many investments, particularly stock and bond portfolios, much easier for individual investors than it may have been decades ago.

As already mentioned, most people don't achieve the best results, but it's certainly not because they aren't smart enough. Successful professionals who routinely accomplish the impossible in their own fields of expertise should be able to do the same with their finances. Yet, it often doesn't seem to unfold that way.

While various challenges that plague investors have already been addressed, the three specific attributes that are likely to have the most influence on the success of any individual in any field boil down to the three characteristics of aptitude, time, and desire. Nearly any person with these three characteristics can become a master. Many people are accustomed to successfully applying these characteristics to other parts of their life, primarily their career. It can be easy for them to assume that they will achieve similar success with their finances.

In my experience, however, many people lack at least one of these three attributes, if not two or three of them. Notice that talent or ability often isn't one of them.

For example, after reading the first part of this book, you probably have enough information to invest in the stock market and achieve a respectable level of success relevant to a reasonable performance bench market. You could probably match or outperform many mutual funds because of your lower costs, or you could choose an approach that simply mimics the stock market. There's enough information in this book to help you also excel in bond markets and potentially identify additional means to diversify a portfolio. Obviously, the material isn't all-inclusive, but ample information is easily accessible over the web or through various experts in different fields who are willing to share their published materials, courses, and workshops. The information is there for those who seek it out. But should you assume this role?

## Aptitude

How good are you at managing your portfolio and specific investments? Be honest. If you have any experience, you probably have some understanding of your abilities. How have you done? Your past performance will probably be the best single predictor of your likely future success.

You may be very good and routinely take actions that benefit you. Market declines may look like opportunities, and you may have capitalized on the stock market drop in 2008 and 2009 by buying equities cheap. But if a market decline drives your blood pressure up and you can't wait for weekends because the markets are closed, you probably are best off avoiding this responsibility.

For many people, emotional issues rule out self-management. Only people who are uniquely wired to overcome natural human tendencies usually have a genuine and predictable capability to manage various investments and integrated portfolios successfully.

While great techniques and practices should make success much more likely, emotionally driven actions tend to inflict far more pain on most portfolios than faulty strategies. There are many exceptions, but the terrible underperformance by investors in the stock and bond markets results primarily from emotionally charged self-sabotage, not terrible investment approaches.

Part of aptitude is expertise. Do you already have it or can you obtain it? Most professionals in any field have a combination of aptitude and expertise. Do you have a system to acquire expertise and continue to enhance your abilities? The world of finance keeps changing, and successful management becomes much more likely if you have consistent access to solid information and practices.

I was reminded of the value of expertise recently when our lawn sprinkler system had a problem. One night, for no apparent reason, the front yard sprinklers started and kept on running. I had to turn off the water to the sprinkler system to stop drenching my lawn.

The previous year, we had had a problem with the same sprinkler zone, and I had replaced the valve, so I knew that I could fix the problem. I also had a better understanding, however, of what was involved.

To start with, our sprinkler valves are buried in the yard with no indication of where they are. It took me at least a full day and multiple 18-inch-deep holes dug through hard clay to find them. By the time I was done, my yard looked as if giant gophers had attacked.

Once I found the water pipes and eventually the valves, I replaced the faulty valves with completely new versions by cutting the old ones off the PVC pipe. To attach the new replacements, I used all kinds of fun things like extra piping, several couplers, primer, glue, and lots of elbow grease. Of course, all these extra hardware pieces and chemicals cost money and took time to find. I searched two Home Depot stores and a Lowe's before I had all the parts.

Finally, once all the pieces were in place and the valves had been tested successfully, I filled back in all my gopher holes. In order to get the ground even as I was replacing the dirt and grass, I soaked the ground with gallons and gallons of water until I was working with mud. I made a real mess, but I got the ground level. After a few weeks, my giant brown patches of grass had turned green again, and my lawn looked great. Mission accomplished.

Now, a year later, when this same valve opened for no reason and stayed open, I was not terribly excited about digging holes, cutting pipe, priming valves, and gluing together new pieces. Once was enough. So this time, I called an expert.

The differences between his approach and mine were comical. The repairman said he would stop by after his full day and take a look. If he could, he would fix it. I was more than a bit skeptical that he could solve a problem in a few minutes that had taken me hours to fix last year.

I was in for a surprise. The repairman arrived around 5:30 p.m. We couldn't find the valves easily because I'd left my location drawings in my office. After spending about a minute poking around in the dirt, he simply attached an electric current generator to another part of the system and found the valves using some type of sensor. I was amazed. It had taken me a least a day's work and numerous gopher holes to do what took him less than five minutes.

Next, he looked at the valves through their housings a few inches below their grass covering rather than digging holes to clear them completely. He determined which valve was bad in about 90 seconds. It was mid-August and very hot, so I went inside, figuring that he might have to come back tomorrow to make the repair. Yet less than 10 minutes later, he knocked on the door to say he was done. The valve was fixed. And, he had tweaked my control box to give me a better watering pattern. It was 5:45, 15 minutes after he'd arrived.

He carried spare parts with him. And instead of cutting off the bad valve from the piping, he simply unscrewed the old valve and replaced the bad internal parts. No digging, no holes, no extra parts, no primer, no glue, no water, and no clay all over my driveway or lawn.

Of course, I had to pay for his services. In return, however, I spent far less money on parts, so my total cost was minimal. He had also adjusted my control unit so that my watering pattern was more appropriate for my yard. And when he was done, my yard looked like a normal, manicured grass lawn instead of a battlefield. I couldn't even tell he'd done anything.

In essence, he had done a better, faster, and more complete job than I ever would have, and most of his fee was offset by the costs he saved me through the services he provided. Over time, our system's better use of water probably more than offset his charges. My entire sprinkler system works better because of the additional changes he made, and my yard looks better.

Experts really can add value. In the world of finance, it may not be as obvious, but access to information, proven systems, sophisticated strategies, and advanced knowledge regarding fees should be factored into your decisions. Do you have this expertise or the ability to acquire it?

If you're still not clear, I've found that a fairly good indicator of ability and expertise tends to be interest. If you have a passion for nearly anything, there's a higher probability that you also have or will develop strong ability in that area. Obviously, interest doesn't guarantee aptitude or experience. Nor does lack of interest mean that you can't do it. But it's another good place to look. Regardless, if you're managing your own funds, you want to be sure you have some natural talent in this area and will quickly develop the appropriate ability.

## Time

Becoming or remaining an expert, or even a relatively informed amateur, requires time. Like seemingly everything else in modern life, the investment world has become more complex, and more commitment is required to stay on top of new developments and opportunities.

Once you've become an expert, managing your investments requires more time. Staying up to date with new investment approaches and tax implications requires attention and dedication. For many if not most people, extra minutes and hours are a difficult commodity to come by. Few casual investors have the slack in their system that is needed to gain expertise and keep their knowledge base updated. For many people, scheduling in the design, implementation, and management of a solid financial strategy is difficult. Most of us are looking for more time in a day rather than more ways to spend it.

Finally, when we do free up extra time, most of us would rather spend it on something other than becoming financial experts and managing our investments. For many, finances are not a favorite activity that naturally gets attention. If most people are blessed with a few free hours, they don't immediately think about spending time with their portfolio.

Again, none of this says that someone cannot develop a solid understanding of investments and manage his money successfully. Rather, most people don't have the desire to become experts or direct their efforts toward this area.

### Desire: Is It Fun or Satisfying?

Let's go back to my sprinkler system. When I fixed my sprinkler system the first time, my desire to complete the job myself was high because my dad was in town. He loves these kinds of projects. Between the two of us, we can fix anything, and it's fun. So, fixing the sprinkler system wasn't a chore that had to be finished, it was a challenge to be conquered.

In addition, to spend time with my dad, I made the time. Fixing the sprinkler system was entertainment. Given other alternative activities, spending time with my dad on a project that we both enjoy was high on my list.

Finally, I had enough aptitude to get the job done. Years earlier, I had spent a summer installing sprinkler systems, and my dad had installed his system completely on his own. Yet, my level of aptitude was the bare minimum needed to complete the project. We made the repair, but we did it the ugly way. We ripped up the lawn and stained the driveway with clay that took months to wash off. An expert would have known better.

We also used lots of extra parts because of our clumsy approach. Our solution was more likely to have future problems because all the extra parts made it a bit less efficient. In fact, one of the valves I had replaced was the same one that broke again.

So what does all this have to do with managing your finances? Well, we already went over the three traits people need if they are to be successful. If we look at these as we did in the sprinkler example, a person must have aptitude and a genuine desire to develop the expertise to become a quasi-financial expert. She should want to manage her finances and should derive a sense of joy and satisfaction from her efforts. When people aspire to understand their finances and administer all their financial affairs, the other pieces, ability and time, tend to fall into place. If I wanted to fix sprinkler systems on a regular basis, my ability would rapidly improve. I already know better than to dig lots of holes.

People with a genuine interest in the financial world are far more likely to learn about different financial possibilities and options. New opportunities and products catch their eye. They pick up the latest dos and don'ts. Random articles capture their attention.

They allocate time to learning and application because they naturally gravitate toward their area of interest. They don't forget or put off action until it's too late. Because this activity is important and enjoyable to them, it gets their attention. They develop expertise and give their financial affairs the attention required. As a result, their portfolio's performance usually reflects their interest and focus.

Someone who is truly interested in financial affairs and who devotes time and energy to managing his portfolio will almost always enjoy more success than someone who views this activity as drudgery, even if this person has lots of aptitude and experience.

This may sound obvious, but most people don't think this through. It's easier for most people to keep doing what they've been doing, whether that's managing their own money or working with a professional.

I saw evidence of this recently when a friend asked me to manager her account. Her husband had been a great friend of mine, and he had passed away after battling cancer. He worked in the financial services industry as a programmer, but had no professional interface with the field of individual investments. Still, he had done an excellent job managing their finances largely because it was his hobby. He genuinely enjoyed devoting time and energy to building a financial future for his family.

His wife also works in the financial services industry and is very familiar with the industry. But, in contrast to her husband, she had no interest in taking over management of her investments in spite of her solid skillset and industry background. She felt much more comfortable working with someone on a professional basis. She recognized that even with her background, she wouldn't put the time or energy in to managing her money that she felt it required. Two equally talented individuals made very different choices because of their interests, not their talent or aptitude.

## Results

There's another commonsense reason that further supports the need to enjoy managing your own portfolio. Statistically, it's highly likely that the largest benefit people get from managing their finances is the enjoyment and satisfaction of doing it themselves. Hopefully, if you choose to manage your own funds, you will achieve success, but statistics suggest otherwise. Obviously, there are exceptions.

There can be other benefits to managing your own money. Some people feel more in control of their money when they're calling all the shots. Others like the flexibility of having all the pieces of their finances solely in their hands. Still others like the speed and privacy that accompany their own management. And there's a myriad of other reasons that someone may want to completely control her finances.

Greater performance through saving on fees and services, however, is often not the best reason to go it alone. Past history and evidence don't support this rationale. In most cases, an investor is better off using some type of outside assistance.

We've already covered several reasons why the average amateur investor may struggle to keep up with professionals. Does the same rationale apply to following a system such as any of those we outlined earlier? Well, let's address this specifically.

I know the information in this book works. Employ an advanced and time-tested portfolio strategy; use an appropriate, high-quality investment vehicle for each asset class; and for stocks, avoid mutual funds in favor of a reliable and cost-efficient stock selection and management system. The validity of this approach has been demonstrated by endowments, further supported by academic studies, and tested against my own experience. If you've made it this far in the book, it's likely that you have the interest and aptitude to apply many if not every one of these principles.

And yet, most people who attempt to implement many of these recommendations, particularly following a particular stock strategy such as the Dow Dividend Strategy, will not have as much success as I would using the exact same system. Even with a clear blueprint including various guidelines and procedures, most people just cannot or will not consistently manage their finances according to a specific plan. This becomes even more applicable when something happens that challenges their current practices. Good management often requires acting too much against our natural self-preservation tendencies.

Furthermore, ongoing management probably requires staying up to date with new developments in addition to putting the time into management. Just as in sprinkler repair, a competent expert has kept up to date with new developments such as the likely location of valves and easy tricks for finding them. In a field as complex as investments, it's logical that someone who devotes his career to the field will have a significant knowledge edge over a casual investor that is likely to increase over time.

My firm has a very senior, full-time employee who is focused almost exclusively on completing due diligence on various investment opportunities. He has access to various third-party due diligence reports that provide extensive details on different aspects of the investments, including comparisons with best-in-class industry standards and reasonable performance expectations for various investments. He regularly attends national conferences and seminars that explore best practices and developments within the industry and across investment products. He is further supported by other personnel and a senior management committee. These people also attend conferences and provide additional viewpoints and checks on potential investments. The opinions, approvals, and intelligence offered by different professionals all provide me with invaluable resources when I am selecting the investments that I believe are best for my clients. In no way does this guarantee success, but it should make it more likely.

In most cases, an individual who is managing her own funds has just the Internet, which offers an incredible wealth of information, but often with no context or vetting by competent and hopefully trusted professionals.

In many cases, an investor who is managing her own money avoids some fees, but also achieves a lower overall portfolio return. Often, amateurs actually pay more in fees through mistakes or missed opportunities than they would if they used an expert. The most obvious example of this is anyone who invests in no-load mutual funds thinking that she's avoiding most of the major costs associated with equity investments. A good financial professional can easily offset all of his charges simply through reducing the fees paid on various investment vehicles. Hopefully, a professional pro-vides more value than that, but many investors can be helped in so many ways that many professionals can easily justify much higher fees than they charge.

It's interesting to note that people with larger portfolios tend to be most likely to understand this concept. Higher-net-worth investors are much more likely to use experts for managing their money than people with smaller portfolios, especially as they grow older and gain experience. An entrepreneur who's done well is more likely to manage his or her own money at age 30 than at age 50. By the time he or she is 50, mistakes have been made, and the value of outside expertise is more appreciated.

So, where does this leave us? Am I saying that I believe no one should invest on his or her own? Absolutely not. Some people do very well flying solo, and many people really enjoy being involved in different investments and building their portfolio. It's a great hobby that can provide very tangible benefits.

My larger point is that the decision to go it alone should be made with the right information and for the right reasons. If you love investments, enjoy the market, know what you're doing, and have the dedication and desire to stick with it, go for it! Investing and managing all aspects of your portfolio can be not only financially rewarding, but also personally satisfying. If you're not terribly interested in investments, however, but you manage your portfolio yourself to avoid paying for assistance, you're probably costing yourself a large amount of money by overvaluing the quality of your own advice.

## Availability

Beyond these considerations, flying solo carries another potential substantial cost. Many of the most valuable investments that endowments add to diversify the performance side of their portfolios are unavailable to individuals without professional assistance. Direct real estate investments, oil and gas partnerships, and private equity, including business development companies, all must be invested in through a licensed registered representative working with a securities firm. While this could change over time as product sponsors work to develop more ways to serve a wider range of investors, current options are limited.

One of the most common substitutes that investors who are going it alone make is using traded REITs instead of direct real estate investments. As mentioned, traded REITs can be a great asset class, but their much greater correlation with stocks and their high volatility, which is more than double that of direct real estate investments, make them a decidedly different asset class, lacking many of the advantage of direct real estate holdings.[1]

If you go it alone, you will still want to diversify your holdings as much as possible in spite of the elimination of all direct investments. Figure 9.1 provides a potential allocation.

**Figure 9.1**  Potential Do-It-Yourself Allocation

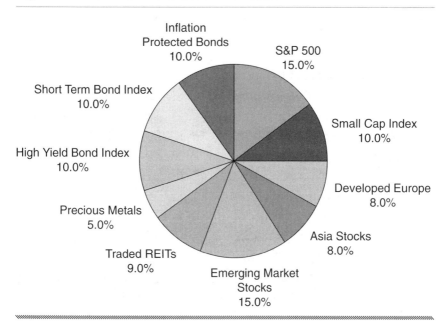

This allocation secures fairly broad diversification by spreading the performance asset allocations across multiple different categories, including different sectors of U.S. equities, international equities, commodities via precious metals, real estate, and high-yield bonds. All these positions are also completely liquid. You could buy them in the morning and sell them in the afternoon.

This portfolio is also easy to implement because all the asset classes and subcategories can be easily invested in through cost-effective vehicles such as exchange-traded funds (ETFs) or index funds. (Note that commodities can be an exception.) If you want to use something more involved, such as the Dow Dividend Strategy or some other trading system, for some of the stock sectors, this portfolio provides the opportunity to integrate these systems into a wider strategy, even if diversification across more assets results in U.S. large-cap stock allocations of only 15 percent.

For all its benefits, the major drawbacks to this portfolio are likely to be the volatility associated with any liquid performance asset and the high levels of correlation among the asset classes. Over time, the various holdings should smooth performance to some degree, but severe market dislocations are likely to hit nearly all the holdings quite hard, with the exception of short-term bonds, inflation-protected bonds, and possibly precious metals.

When investors are most nervous, resulting in the largest market drops, many of the subsector equity asset classes plummet even faster than the large-cap S&P 500 index. In 2008, the S&P 500 lost 37 percent, but traded REITs lost nearly 41 percent, developed market stocks lost more than 43 percent, and emerging market stocks lost more than 50 percent.[2]

It's not that this portfolio will not work, but sophisticated institutions purposely take a very different approach. Their strategies target much higher risk-adjusted returns that are much more independent of the whims of the stock market. Still, if you want to fly solo, and you have the discipline to manage through the inevitable market declines, this portfolio can provide a solid starting point.

If you need income, the inclusion of high-yield bonds and traded REITs in this portfolio would probably increase the portfolio's dividend yield about 10 to 15 percent above that of a 60/40 stock/bond portfolio, but it will probably fall well short of the yields produced by a portfolio that more closely resembles that of an endowment. Since this portfolio is 100 percent liquid, you have many choices of assets to sell to supplement dividends. Just keep in mind that the correlation among most of these holdings probably means that you really have only three separate asset classes—stocks, bonds, and precious metals—to choose from.

If you're ready to fly solo, the information we've covered should make you a more effective investor and help you achieve your desired success. If you think you might like some additional help, the next chapter explores how to choose a financial partner wisely.

## 10

# Profitable Partnering

ENDOWMENTS, INSTITUTIONS, AND VERY HIGH NET WORTH investors virtually always depend heavily on experts and specialists to help them create and manage their portfolios. Similarly, nearly every professional athlete uses at least one coach to help them reach their greatest potential.

For the last couple of years, my family has hosted in our home a young lady golfer who is on the equivalent of the women's futures tour. She is working to move up to the top league, the Ladies Professional Golf Association (LPGA). Gaining a much greater insight into the world of golf, including the tremendous network of coaches, tools, and resources that she and others use routinely, has been very interesting. She has a swing coach, a strength training coach, a physical therapy coach to address old injuries, and other experts that she uses on a less frequent basis to deal with more specific issues such as strategy, diet, or game management.

Her use of coaches resembles the practices employed by most wealthy individuals, who use an advisor for investments, a CPA for taxes, an estate planning attorney for legacy planning, bankers for borrowing, and other specialists for more particular needs. Just as some athletes use more than one coach, some investors may have one advisor to help with more traditional assets, such as stocks and bonds, and another advisor to help with the more rapidly developing world of alternative investments.

Many people and organizations are very willing to help you manage your money. As in nearly any field, however, some advisors are much better than others, and each will be a bit different because they're people, not machines. Your own needs and likes will play a major role in choosing someone, as will your own personality. Even the best advisor may not be a good fit for you if you don't like or respect him or her.

In any event, you want to be sure to choose a highly competent advisor who can help you continually clarify and achieve your goals. Retirees, in particular, have a lot riding on their choice because most of them don't have employment income available to replace lost savings resulting from bad advice.

While there's no standard definition of the perfect financial advisor, there are several basic areas to look at when seeking out a financial partner.

## Hard and Soft Skills

When you are seeking an advisor, you obviously want someone who will make it much more likely that you will achieve your financial goals. Most of the skills that will provide you as an investor with value are hard skills, such as experience, knowledge, relevant expertise, and emotional discipline. Fortunately, a bit of research reveals competence in most of these areas pretty quickly.

While these skills are very important, however, most investors tend to choose their advisor based more on soft, or people, skills. Trust nearly always tops the list, followed in some way by comfort or likability. It is well known in the financial services industry that an advisor who has excellent people and marketing abilities will nearly always achieve much greater success than a more skilled and experienced advisor who lacks the nonfinancial marketing and people skills. It's a relationship business. Your trust in an advisor will make decisions, actions, and ongoing management much easier, but a higher probably of success is still likely to result from specific skills, not just ability with people.

When you are choosing an advisor, you have to successfully deal with the need to trust and like your advisor. You are a person who will be working with a person, and, unlike a doctor's appointment, your meetings will probably last well beyond just a few minutes. And besides, trying to turn this process into a purely analytical event sucks all the fun out of starting a new and hopefully very profitable relationship.

With this in mind, the next sections provide some straight-forward guidance on what to look for in a financial advisor and where you might be most likely to find someone who meets your needs. Finding the right person can a bit like fishing. If you start in the right place with the right tools, immediate success isn't guaranteed, but it becomes far more likely that you will catch something a lot faster.

## Experience

There is simply no substitute for experience. Out of all the different characteristics to look at in an advisor, this area easily ranks far above everything else. You want to be sure that your potential advisor has been in the business for several years and has seen ups and downs in the economy and in the market. A potential advisor should have been in the business long enough to have made mistakes on other people and, as a result, to have gained some caution and restraint. He or she should be familiar with a wide range of products, and should understand the ins and outs of working with different product vendors and companies.

For most advisors, the minimum amount of experience required is 5 years, and 10 years or more of relevant and meaningful experience is obviously better. This is not at all unreasonable, although a requirement of even 5 years of experience will eliminate many financial professionals. This doesn't mean that you can work only with people over the age of 50. There are good advisors who are in their thirties and even some who are in their twenties. If you're working with someone younger, however, find out where he's spent his career. If he's been in the financial services industry for only a couple of years and has never gone through some real ups and downs, you will probably be better served by another advisor. The likelihood of such an advisor learning on you is simply too high.

You might wonder how anyone new gets started in the business. Well, first, this is neither your problem nor your responsibility. Please do not let a kind heart lead you into becoming someone's test case. You don't want someone learning on you. Second, if someone really wants to become an expert in the business, she usually works with a more experienced person for years to build her knowledge base. In fact, many people work in teams to ensure that a high level of experience and expertise is available to the client in an environment that benefits everyone.

If someone is out on his own or works by himself in his own office, make sure he's been flying solo for at least a couple of years. Immediately after leaving a large company with many resources and restrictions, people are more likely to make mistakes because they're learning how to service clients in a completely new manner with different resources and tools. Again, if someone is going to make mistakes, you want him to have been learning while advising someone else early in his career. By ensuring that he's got at least a minimal amount of experience, your likelihood of good advice and service increases substantially.

Experience also demonstrates a commitment to the industry. The financial services industry has a tremendously high washout rate. Many people like the concept of working in the money field and think it would be great to work around finances all day. Once they get into the business, many of them find that they're not really well suited to working with individual investors while developing and maintaining expertise on multiple approaches, products, and practices. Success in the industry requires strong technical knowledge and an ability to work with people.

Finally, an advisor should not only have experience in the markets and in managing money, but also have specific experience handling the type of client that you would be. For instance, if you are a retiree or will be one soon, you want to make sure that your potential planner has significant experience addressing the common issues that are specific to retirees, such as experience in harvesting a portfolio.

In fact, most people find that the best relationships are with someone who specializes in their particular niche. If you're 40 years old with three kids, your financial concerns will be largely dictated by your stage in life. You'll be focused on planning for your children's educations, preliminary retirement planning (hopefully), home mortgage rates, budgeting your expenses, life insurance, and maximizing your investment returns. College savings programs and housing payments will be high on your list. Areas of importance to the average retiree, such as stable portfolio income, required minimum distributions, estate planning, social security benefits, outliving your money, and long-term care, are probably not even a concern unless you're caring for an aging parent.

Assuming that you intend to build a portfolio that includes alternative assets adds an additional qualification to your advisor's experience. While the field has been expanding rapidly for many years, a surprisingly small number of advisors have a strong background in this area. This has partly hindered the model's growth, although this is changing. People with strong expertise across these different areas definitely exist. You may need to do a bit of research, however, to find the right person.

## Knowledge and Expertise

Just as you want your advisor to have applicable experience, she should also have the right kind of knowledge and expertise. While applicable experience is likely to result in the desired knowledge, this isn't a given. Assuming that you want someone to help you build a portfolio more similar to that of an endowment, your advisor will need strong experience with both traditional assets such as stocks and bonds and newer alternative assets.

Most advisors that work with larger and more sophisticated accounts eschew mutual funds for their stock and bond strategies in favor of newer and more efficient strategies or vehicles. This isn't a requirement, as some mutual funds and index mutual funds offer excellent value, but an advisor's use of a mediocre investment vehicle should send up red flags that need further investigation. In any event, your advisor should have a solid and time-tested approach to traditional asset classes.

When looking for someone with a good background in alternatives, you will need to be a bit more realistic. Finding someone with decades of experience dealing with debt and private equity business development companies (BDCs) will be impossible. The category really didn't become a viable option for individual investors until 2009. Nontraded REITs have been around for decades, but their popularity didn't really increase until after the go-go years of the 1990s, when individuals first began looking for performance assets other than stocks.

Similarly, the industry continues to evolve rapidly, so almost no one will be an expert in all areas. You want to avoid, however, anyone who gives you a blank stare and tells you that he will get back to you with some information. Again, you don't want to be anyone's developmental test case.

You can approach this area much the way you would finding a doctor. Just as in medicine, financial professionals specialize because of the incredible complexity of the field. An advisor simply can't be all things to all people. This can be both bad and good. If you talk to a financial professional who specializes in insurance products, every need you may have will probably be met with an annuity. Similarly, a professional trained only in the use of mutual funds will probably create financial solutions that essentially mimic a 60/40 stock/bond portfolio using only mutual funds.

Most likely, your needs will be best met by the financial advisor equivalent of an experienced and knowledgeable general practitioner. An advisor serving in this capacity will understand how to create a portfolio and then implement it by outsourcing specific activities to experts. Like a doctor utilizing specialists, most advisors depend on outside third-party advisors to manage stocks, bonds, and various alternatives. Just as you probably wouldn't want your general practitioner performing heart surgery on you, you probably don't want your advisor providing specialty services such as stock picking.

The knowledge and expertise of your advisor will show up in two primary areas. First, can the advisor design a portfolio that meets your specific needs? The number of available tools has skyrocketed in recent years, providing advisors with more tools than ever to create highly advanced and customized portfolios.

Second, once a general design has been created, the advisor must use his or her knowledge of third-party vendors to choose specific products and services for the different asset classes in your portfolio. For years, many advisors simply used a couple of different mutual fund families to meet all their needs. The world is moving past this, particularly for higher-net-worth individuals, but not all advisors have made the transition. The larger number of categories in an endowment model portfolio demands more expertise. Even if you personally connect with someone, if the advisor's portfolio design or knowledge of third-party vendors, particularly of alternatives, doesn't inspire confidence, hopefully, you will keep looking.

## Emotional Discipline

Given the importance of controlling one's emotions while managing a portfolio, any successful advisor should have the ability to not only control his or her own emotions, but help you control yours as well. While most people in the industry excel in this area, since it's such a fundamental requirement for success, you will want to be confident that this person can keep both of you on track during the inevitable ups and downs.

A superior portfolio design makes this much easier, but it doesn't guarantee success. A quick discussion regarding the advisor's practices and client management during the 2008 meltdown should provide some pretty good background. While no one is going to tell you that he panicked and told his clients to sell at the bottom, any discussion should make you feel more comfortable that his approach will make you emotionally more comfortable before and during any crisis, since economic and stock market downturns will happen.

While emotional discipline may be a hard skill, you can't really measure it. You will probably judge an advisor as competent or not based on your level of trust. The advisor will either earn it or not.

### Licenses

The type of licenses an advisor holds can provide one of the easiest means to determine if a financial professional is a good fit for you. Much as you would seek out an orthopedic surgeon rather than a dentist for a knee injury, various licenses in the financial services industry indicate particular training and expertise. You will still need to use your judgment, however. Just as most orthopedic surgeons believe that every injury requires surgery rather than physical therapy or chiropractic care, advisors with specific licenses and backgrounds can also believe that their approach must be the answer to every question.

If you are seeking to implement a portfolio similar to that of an endowment, you will almost certainly require a dually licensed advisor. While this could change depending on new regulations and product offerings, current regulations require a securities license (Series 7, or registered representative) to offer direct investments, including most alternatives, and an advisory license (Series 65 or 66, or investment advisor representative) to offer fee-based stock and bond managed accounts. There can be exceptions, such as a registered representative using mutual funds for stocks and bonds, but generally, a dually licensed professional has the most flexibility to choose the best options for nearly any portfolio. In addition, there can be advantages to holding an insurance license for some specific guaranteed products. This license is not required to build an endowment model portfolio, but some advisors incorporate guaranteed annuities into the more conservative portion of a portfolio.

The financial services industry has continually tried to help investors engage with financial professionals easily according to clear rules. Unfortunately, technology changes and unintended consequences of additional regulations have often confused investors rather than enlightening them.

A decade or more ago, the industry began moving toward a fee-based model and away from brokers who sold stocks for a commission. In the fee-based model, fee-based advisors charge their clients a fee for assets under management rather than charging commissions on trades, as is required under the brokerage model. Many professionals and individual investors saw the new fee-based model as superior because both advisors and their clients benefited when portfolios performed well and suffered when they performed poorly. The arrangement's emphasis on end results over trading also appealed to clients and professionals because the incentives seemed better aligned. In addition, from a professional's perspective, the fee-based arrangement required much less regulatory oversight, and running a business under this arrangement is normally simpler and much less expensive. The arrangement seemed to represent the future, and most people assumed that nearly all professionals helping individual investors would eventually work under it.

But the 2008 meltdown and the rapid growth of alternatives upset many of these assumptions. In order for an advisor to charge a fee on an investment, the investment usually must be highly liquid, which automatically eliminates nearly all alternatives. Performance has also been a problem. During the financial meltdown, nearly all liquid assets other than government bonds performed even worse than the U.S. stock market. Diversification into almost anything other than government bonds actually hurt investors, and a large percentage of fee-based advisors suffered horrible years as their clients' portfolios plunged.

By contrast, many if not most alternatives, which are available only through more traditional brokerage channels, performed much better than fully liquid securities. After the meltdown, it became much more difficult for fee-only advisors to blindly tout the superiority of their model, given their often dismal performance. An arrangement that was created to benefit individual investors now seems to unintentionally restrict many professionals, resulting in their having less flexibility to offer the best products and services available.

The last downturn has increased the pressure on regulators to develop a uniform standard that is more intuitively understandable to investors, but progress remains slow. Much of the debate centers on the fiduciary standard. Fee-based advisors are required to act in their clients' best interest as a fiduciary, while brokers are required only to provide products that are suitable for a particular investor. Changes in the suitability standard in mid-2012 make the two guidelines almost identical, but there are still minor distinctions that result in completely different regulatory rules, regulators, structures, practices, and allowable compensation structures.

A licensed registered representative can sell you a nontraded REIT, while a fee-based advisor usually cannot because the fee-based advisor can charge a fee only on something that is actively managed. Because a nontraded REIT requires a time commitment by the investor, and the fee-based advisor cannot advise a client to sell it, regulations prohibit the advisor from charging a fee for advice because there is no advice to give once the product has been bought.

These restrictions result in some odd circumstances. The industry is trying to develop offerings that allow more liquidity, yet the product changes often result in clearly reduced target returns and greater volatility. Most professionals, including the purveyors of the products, admit that the newer products are inferior, or at least offer a poorer risk/reward trade-off. But, because the fee-based advisor can advise a client to liquidate these investments, he or she can recommend the investment to a client. Ironically, in this case, the fee-based advisor is supposedly acting in the client's best interest as a fiduciary, but is recommending a product that explicitly targets lower returns with greater volatility. I don't make the rules; I just live by them.

The rapid evolution of the alternatives space caught much of the industry by surprise. Many fee-only advisors adopted the new fee-based business model, believing that they were acting in their clients' best interests while also solving a thorny regulatory problem.

Unfortunately, the industry's movement toward alternatives has left many of these advisors in the lurch. It's expensive to add back dropped licenses and gain an affiliation with a broker/dealer, and if you have been out of the industry for any length of time, most high-quality broker/dealers will not allow you to affiliate with them.

Many financial professionals retained their licenses so that they could maintain access to nearly any product. Investment advisory licenses allow them to offer fee-based services for many offerings, such as stocks and bonds, and brokerage licenses enable them to provide commission-based services for investments such as alternatives.

The design of most alternatives also precludes some of the perceived problems that existed with more traditional commission products. With stocks and bonds, brokers made money only when their clients traded, so the obvious incentive was to sell someone on a new idea, whether it helped the client's portfolio or not.

Alternatives are different. Once you buy them, the broker has no control over when the product will be fully liquid again. The advisor can't sell you on a new idea because you generally can't sell the old investment even if you want to. While the broker still makes money when you invest just like the fee-only advisor does, there is no perverse incentive to churn an account. The incentives for fee-based accounts and most alternatives are now quite similar, and annual compensation is also designed to be about the same.

In addition, professional conduct requirements are also converging to nearly the same standard in spite of inaction by regulators. As well as recent changes that require brokers to adhere to standards that are very similar to the investment advisory fiduciary standard, if a broker working under the suitability rules offers you any services that include a fee, all of his recommendations to you will be required to meet the fiduciary standard of acting in your best interest. Many would also argue that much tighter regulations and audits of brokers than of investment advisors probably result in tighter adherence to standards.

The distinction between different capabilities and licenses becomes more meaningful when it is applied to potential recommendations that a professional can make. The portfolio presented in Figure 9.1 as a possible portfolio solution for an individual who is flying solo could easily represent the best recommendation of an advisor who is licensed only as a fee-based advisor. It offers great diversification across multiple liquid asset classes and should provide solid risk-adjusted returns given the constraints of working only with liquid securities. Yet, for multiple reasons that have already been well covered, I believe a more advanced portfolio structure offers vastly superior performance for a given level of risk, while also providing greater income and flexibility for someone who is in or near retirement. But, in order to recommend this portfolio, the advisor would need to hold a securities license (Series 7). A dually licensed advisor can choose among the best products and services available from any source.

The industry has been moving in this direction for many years as financial professionals seek to offer comprehensive services to their clients. Yet, there is still a movement within the industry that claims that fee-only structures must be superior to everything else because of the compensation arrangement. While the structure has obvious benefits, the prohibition on using so many valuable investments automatically eliminates it as a serious option for most investors, given current regulatory restrictions. I believe the arrangement places the ideology of the advisor above the reality of the marketplace because it forces the elimination of many of the best options available from many of the world's best providers of investments who are already working with institutions and endowments. Very simply, it ignores the practical needs of clients.

If you are working to find a new advisor, the licenses held by an advisor provide a quick and simple screen of potential candidates

## Types of Companies

Just as professionals differ by licenses and focus areas, many of them adopt specific business models that enable them to deliver their customized services more easily. Numerous business models exist throughout the industry, and the financial meltdown that dragged many firms' names through the mud further changed the industry by making it less desirable for many financial professionals to keep their affiliation with the large, established name-brand firms.

## Big-Name Firms

Larger firms with recognizable names tend to have more controls and procedures in place that all their advisors must follow. Often, they have stricter compliance rules and manage their brokers according to specific requirements. In addition, many of their brokers are on the younger side. Big firms often provide great training for new brokers that ensures basic levels of service regardless of how qualified the individual may or may not be.

Larger firms generally provide easier access to a greater variety of expertise. If you need estate planning or a living will, or if you would like easy access to your funds on frequent international trips, a large firm will probably provide these services more readily than a regional or small company.

The size and structures of large firms usually assure you of a standard set of services, complete with a basic level of competence. It's unlikely that recommendations are going to be completely off base or overexpose you to inappropriate levels of risk.

But these firms suffer from several significant downsides. You are far more likely to get a standard recommendation from a relatively inexperienced broker who is following unimaginative company guidelines. Large brokerage firms often give their brokers very specific instructions on exactly what strategies to follow and what stocks to buy, and forbid them from acting otherwise. Tight regulations and stiff fines for perceived infractions give firms strong incentives to limit the possibility that a recommendation could be construed as inappropriate. Most larger firms address this challenge by forcing their brokers to adhere to more simplistic, standardized models.

This can be good because you're less likely to receive awful advice, but it can also be highly limiting. You're more likely to get the standard investment approach that provides you with unimaginative, stodgy returns.

The larger problem is nearly always access to alternative investments. Many of these firms have their own investment units that offer their own versions of alternatives. Their offerings are nearly always some type of hedge fund. When direct investments are available, the offerings usually come in the form of much smaller and riskier private placements that are available only to accredited investors. Again, these offerings nearly always come from the firm's investment banking unit or some other internal department that does not compete with the much larger stable of independent offerings because the independents are not allowed through the door. It's very rare that offerings will include investment programs from outside the company. They are not profitable enough. Any money directed their way reduces the funds flowing to more profitable internal products. This limitation makes it very difficult to implement an endowment model strategy using a traditional big-name investment firm.

## Boutique Firms

Smaller boutique firms often specialize in particular types of clients or services, and can provide a great match for investors who are seeking their particular area of expertise. Their focus helps them differentiate themselves from other financial professionals, and their specialization often makes them ideal for a person who fits their mold.

Most of these firms are run by their owners. Since these companies were often founded because of the strong convictions of the partner or partners, the firms' passion for what they do often shows through in their service and conviction. Most of the owners didn't need to start the company, but they did so because they believed they could offer their clients better solutions and services through their own firm than they could by working for a large company. There's no guarantee that they will succeed, because they have often forsaken advanced infrastructures and various resources in order to start the company, but their conviction that they are offering the absolute best for their clients can make them excellent partners.

Many of these types of firms went independent to gain complete control over the types of investments they recommend. If the office has grown beyond a couple of people, these professionals nearly always have solid experience because they probably spent several years with a larger firm before starting their own firm. Since these firms often originate because of a passion to offer clients a better solution, they tend to have much greater expertise in alternatives. Very small one- or two-person offices can also offer good services, but it tends to be tougher for them because the principals must be experts in everything from products to paperwork.

The range of competence in firms of this type is the greatest by far. Some people have gone the independent route to give themselves greater freedom in servicing their clients and meeting their own lifestyle desires. They may have developed strong expertise and an excellent network of professionals that provide excellent services. Their advice and approach may be fantastic for your needs.

However, the financial professionals who basically resemble semi-competent small-time real estate agents with little focus and scattered expertise are nearly always independents too. In my experience, this type of advisor tends to know a bit about a lot of things, with a primary focus on peddling mutual funds to small investors. Fortunately, this tends to be pretty obvious immediately, and avoiding these people is usually pretty easy.

Since nearly all boutique and specialty firms focus either on a particular customer type or on the products and services offered, an experienced boutique firm that is focused on services close to your needs frequently will be your best option. Their independence gives them the widest access to products and services, and their smaller size often enables them to easily adapt superior solutions using more advanced practices.

There are two primary categories of independents, and dually licensed professionals represent both. Independents who hold a Series 7 license may be affiliated with a broker/dealer. These professionals are technically called registered representatives (RRs), but the older term was broker. Now, they are most often referred to as advisors. Fee-only advisors are technically investment advisor representatives, although they are also usually referred to as advisors.

Independents who are associated with broker/dealers are often highly independent, but they still must adhere to the rules and regulations of the broker/dealer that supervises them. In addition, they will probably have access to the broker/dealer's pool of experts and can draw on the talent available through this association. In addition, oversight by a corporate office hopefully makes sure that an advisor is not incompetent or unethical. The structure exists and helps assure minimum service and competence.

A fee-only advisor may or may not have a company affiliation. Some are licensed as fee-only investment advisor representatives by the state. Others choose to be licensed under a corporate investment advisory firm, just as registered representatives do through their broker/dealer. An independent, fee-based investment advisor operates with extremely limited oversight. As of 2012, the average advisor is audited only once every 11 years, compared with the biannual audits of broker/dealers.[1] In many states, obtaining a license requires little more than filling out a few pieces of paper. This doesn't mean that these people will be unethical or incompetent, but if they are, no one other than you is likely to figure this out.

Unfortunately, the split in the road that has made alternatives mostly off limits to fee-only RIAs eliminates many highly qualified professionals from consideration. As product designs and regulations evolve, this may change and open up a larger group of professionals for consideration. But for now, these fee-only advisors are almost like the part of the group that followed a path that led to the wrong side of the river, and now are wondering if and when they can cross back over to join the main group. They either have to go back and pick up more licenses or hope that regulations change and provide them with a bridge that will let them access alternatives.

With all the smaller boutique and specialty firms, you want to be sure that your needs correspond to their focus. If the firm really specializes, it will probably not accept you as a client if your needs and its focus do not correspond unless there are extenuating circumstances such as family relationships or estate management issues.

Don't force a fit if there isn't one, even if you know the firm provides excellent service to its present clientele.

Of course, smaller size and independence also have a downside. Just because passionate founders try to offer the absolute best solutions does not guarantee that they can or will do so. Fewer restraints and more options can result in superior solutions, but problems can be more likely, too. The talent and abilities of the individual partners become a much greater determinant of the quality of the firm's services.

Basic due diligence about a professional's experience, expertise, and licenses reveals a lot. Many will provide referrals if asked, but be careful about trusting in them too much. In my experience, clients will tell you great things about an advisor if they like that advisor, regardless of his or her actual competence or success. The receipt of a birthday card every year may overly color someone's perception of his or her advisor's abilities.

## Certifications and Awards

Initials after an advisor's name often act as a double-edged sword. Just as the industry has tried to standardize and simplify advice through more licensing and regulation, various institutions have tried to elevate the profession through more advanced education and the creation of credentials that communicate a professional's minimal level of expertise. Obviously, more education and information can be helpful, as they assure a basic level of competence and commitment. Yet a certification doesn't guarantee good advice or service any more than a driver's license guarantees good driving habits.

If you've gone through the previous steps of screening for experience, expertise, and licenses, this area is not nearly as important as those with certifications would like you to believe. If your potential advisor doesn't have any significant certifications, this isn't necessarily a reason to eliminate him or her. It just means that you'll need to dig a bit deeper elsewhere. Certifications are not totally irrelevant, but you're probably better off emphasizing other areas.

The Certified Financial Planner (CFP) designation is probably the most meaningful and common certification for advisors working with individual investors. To obtain this certification, CFPs must study and pass examinations in risk management, investments, tax planning, retirement planning, and estate planning. CFPs must also have a minimum of three years' work experience. In addition, they must continue to update their knowledge in the field and adhere to a prescribed code of ethics. Probably the biggest downside of this designation has been the organization's implicit emphasis on fee-only planning as a business model. While this focus has diminished in recent years, unfortunately too many CFPs went with the original choice and offer more limited services because of their licenses.

Another common certification is the ChFC, or Chartered Financial Consultant. ChFCs must complete courses in economics, investments, insurance, taxation, and related areas from the American College in Bryn Mawr, Pennsylvania. There is also an experience requirement of three years, but the experience does not need to be related to financial advising or planning in any way, making it less meaningful. This designation is an outgrowth of the Chartered Life Underwriter (CLU) program, which indicates extensive study in insurance.

A designation that is more common among accountants is the PFS, or Personal Financial Specialist. Additional specialized education in the area of financial planning is needed, and accountants must also meet a three-year experience requirement.

Other certifications include Accredited Financial Counselor (AFC). The Association for Financial Counseling and Planning Education provides this certification to people who pass examinations in personal finance and financial counseling, as well as follow the AFC code of ethics.

Chartered Financial Analyst (CFA) designations are awarded by the CFA Institute (formerly the Association for Investment Management and Research, or AIMR) after examinations at three different levels. For example, the first level includes such areas as understanding investment analysis and management, financial markets, portfolio management, and securities law.

The Chartered Alternative Investment Analyst (CAIA) is a newer certification that is experiencing rapid growth given the explosion of the alternatives sector. It's a difficult certification to earn, and its value often steers professionals toward very large portfolios. As a result, many of the individuals who have this certification work primarily with very high net worth investors. The certification is slowly trickling down to advisors serving smaller investors.

The Five Star Wealth Manager is an award that has grown in prestige over the past few years. It recognizes wealth managers who help their clients prepare a financial plan and/or implement aspects of their financial plan and can include individuals with various licenses. The nomination and selection criteria are quite rigorous. Ten eligibility and evaluation criteria are used to assess the quality of services provided to clients. Less than 7 percent of financial professionals in a geographic area receive the award.

You might be wondering how you can sort through all this alphabet soup. The easiest way to approach certifications is to seek out those that are most relevant. Of those listed here, the CFP certification and Five Star Wealth Managers are probably most applicable to the average person seeking financial advice.

One last certification also deserves some attention. It's obvious, yet it is often overlooked. Find out what the advisor studied in school and what level of education he attained. While an MBA or PhD in finance will not guarantee good individual financial advice, it's probably an indication that the advisor has a longstanding interest in the topic and will base his decisions on solid principles. Academia is often ahead of industry in the financial world because the performance of investments is so dependent upon sophisticated research, theories, and mathematical models. A solid understanding of portfolio theory, statistics, diversification, and other issues can help an advisor make sounder decisions. Advanced education in finance can be a real plus.

With all that said, however, be careful about making this issue a hurdle that screens out qualified candidates. Many financial professionals have gone through extensive training programs with their companies that approximate the certification programs listed here.

If you're at all concerned that a potential advisor doesn't have a certification that you would rather he had, ask him about the issue directly. Have him explain to you why it's not a problem that he isn't a CFP, CAIA, ChFC, PFS, AFC, CLU, MBA, or whatever it is you'd feel better about him having. Then listen to his answer. If his explanation makes sense to you and you're comfortable, great. If you're not convinced, move on.

## Portfolio Size

Yes, size does matter, at least for your portfolio. Having more money generally opens up better options. Better advisors tend to focus on assisting individuals with larger amounts of money. It's simple economics. Regulatory costs and requirements have mushroomed many times over during the past decades, and shrinking margins usually steer better advisors away from smaller portfolios. If you don't have much now, there are still good options, but your approach to finding a professional will probably need to differ from that of someone with a much larger portfolio.

### Larger Portfolios

Before we start, let's add a bit more clarity to the term *larger portfolio*. Liquid assets of $250,000 does not define a large portfolio by almost any firm's standards, and many advisors will not work with someone until he has $500,000 or $1,000,000 in net worth. I've started at $250,000, however, because under current regulations, a portfolio of this size is large enough to access most investments, excluding those that require accredited investor status. Generally, a larger portfolio basically means a portfolio that's large enough to get the attention of someone who has substantial experience, is probably a bit more qualified, and exceeds minimum regulatory requirements. Please note that regulations change over time, making these levels moving targets.

If you're in this range, you can find someone to match your needs if you are willing to put a bit of effort into the search. While your general needs will not be the same as someone else's, there are several characteristics of an advisor that you'll want regardless of your specific requirements.

You want an advisor who manages your money through a well-defined plan based on an asset allocation strategy with characteristics similar to an endowment's. The quality of this high-level plan will probably be the largest influence on the success of your finances. The specific vehicles you choose for specific categories, such as U.S. stocks or direct real estate, will also affect your returns, but probably by much less than your original strategy development.

I read once, but can't remember where, that only 3.0 percent of investors with portfolios less than $500,000 have a written plan in place by which they manage their money. In contrast, 97 percent of investors with portfolios in excess of $10 million follow a written plan. Since I read this around the turn of the century, the numbers have certainly changed. While I'm not sure if these numbers are still accurate, my experience suggests that the numbers are similar.

At the core of nearly every plan is an asset allocation strategy like the one endowments employ that clearly outlines asset class selection and how allocation will be adjusted as their values inevitably change.

Larger portfolios provide the advisor with more options to exercise his skill in diversification to your benefit. Financial advisors who work with larger portfolios tend to have much greater expertise in diversifying across asset classes using various products and services, and you'll want to seek them out.

As part of ongoing management, an advisor should rebalance your portfolio on an as-needed basis. If an asset has grown or decreased in value to such an extent that it differs significantly from its original target allocation, you want your advisor to buy or sell some of this asset until its target percentage is restored. With some asset classes, such as real estate or private equity, selling assets to buy depressed stocks can be difficult or even impossible because they are not liquid. But other techniques such as redirecting income can be used, and an experienced professional will have multiple techniques that can make ongoing management more successful.

In addition, more experienced advisors specializing in larger portfolios are probably more likely to learn about and take advantage of new opportunities. Many of the best products available today didn't even exist five years ago, and this trend has been true for years. Developments within finance may not be as rapid as those in consumer electronics, but they're closer than you may think. Finding an advisor to help you stay informed of new developments will add tremendous value to your portfolio.

If you are working with a dually licensed professional, which tends to be more common for advisors working with larger portfolios, she will probably use both fee-based and commission-based products and services. Because many of the best stock and bond strategies are available through fee-only arrangements, many advisors use this arrangement for equities and fixed income. As mentioned, most alternatives are currently available only through a brokerage firm on a commission basis, so including them requires working on a commission basis.

For a larger portfolio, it's much easier to find a good advisor who avoids mutual funds. Given the horrible performance of mutual funds relative to the market, it should be obvious that advice to invest in these securities is rarely worth the additional fees. Because mutual funds were designed for much smaller accounts, and their main advantage was often investors' ability to make small contributions cheaply, few advisors specializing in larger accounts use them.

## Smaller Portfolios

If your portfolio is smaller than $250,000, your portfolio design must be adjusted to eliminate nearly all alternatives. After the 1986 tax reform, which saw many investors lose large amounts of money in tax shelters of various types, state regulators enacted minimum-net-worth requirements for various types of direct invest-ments. If you are a smaller investor, you can put all your money in a single small-cap stock, but you can't diversify your portfolio using most alternatives. Again, I don't make the rules; I just follow them.

A portfolio similar to the one outlined in Figure 9.1 could work well for you, but you may want to adjust your holdings up and down to reflect your specific goals and circumstances.

Beyond portfolio design, the biggest differences you'll face from the situation of someone with a larger portfolio will come down to competence and service.

You will probably have a smaller pool of competent advisors to choose from because the best advisors often focus on managing larger portfolios. Larger portfolios present more opportunities and more challenges, and, of course, pay better. Better advisors tend to gravitate toward the bigger fish. This doesn't mean, however, that you can't find a competent advisor, or convince an advisor who usually swims with bigger fish to let you tag along. There are very good advisors who set no minimums on portfolio size and truly enjoy helping investors of any size. You can find them, but it will probably take more effort.

Perhaps a bigger issue may be the level of service you're likely to receive. An investor with an eight-figure portfolio can expect a good strategic plan, accompanied by thorough implementation and diligent ongoing management. His expert advisor will be readily available, and good performance reports will be provided regularly. Over time, the strategy will be adjusted to include new developments and evolving needs.

This level of service may not be routine with a smaller portfolio. It's not that companies can't or won't provide this service. It's more likely that it's not automatic or free. The technology and personnel required to deliver outstanding service are expensive, and the fees generated by small portfolios may not be enough to cover the costs.

If you have parents or close friends who can get you in the door of a firm that might normally be off limits, this can be a great way to both find and receive services that might not normally be available to you. Good advisors can be like doctors who rarely accept new patients. You may need to use other resources to get in the door if you can't dangle a large portfolio in front of someone.

If your portfolio is smaller, finding someone to develop and implement a customized solution may be more challenging. Frequently, more standardized portfolio designs are applied to smaller portfolios. This is no problem if your needs are fairly straightforward, and smaller portfolios often preclude the use of many investments anyway. Your particular idiosyncrasies, however, are less likely to be serviced. If you have a unique need, an hourly fee basis may be more appropriate to ensure that you receive the advice you want rather than the advice someone wants to provide.

You may be able to find a specialty firm that matches your needs. However, these firms are more likely to have investment minimums that could preclude any relationship. Regardless, this is a good place to start.

If that doesn't work, look for the nearest thing to a specialist at any size firm. It will be easier to sort through more people faster if you start at the larger firms, but you may be shuttled from one beginner to another. Independent financial advisors are always an option, and can be a particularly good match for people with smaller accounts. As we covered before, however, you really need to look at the quality of the advisor before going forward.

## Getting Started

If you're just getting started building a portfolio, your options will be limited, but the Internet and many readily available resources from companies can make creating and managing a portfolio surprisingly easy. Going it alone until you build up some assets may be your only choice. Nearly all of the big mutual fund companies offer many resources online or over the phone. They can be a great resource, since their strength is helping small investors build up assets through steady, small contributions.

For many small investors, big firms can also be a good approach. The larger firm will "carry" an unprofitable (i.e., very small) client in hopes that someday, she will become a larger and therefore profitable account. In addition, the controls regarding basic services should ensure that you receive relatively appropriate advice. The area to be careful about is matching your needs to the firm's services. Many large firms will try to sell expensive and completely worthless financial plans to unsuspecting investors. The plans are purposely so complicated that you have to use the firm's services to interpret the results, and thus you're already out several hundred dollars before you even start investing.

Fortunately, most of the big mutual fund companies are more interested in selling you their products than in selling you complex plans. You can start with a simplified version of Figure 9.1 and add to it as you accumulate more assets.

## Referrals

Referrals can be a great way to find an advisor, but be careful. Although this may be a comfortable method for many people, it has two major pitfalls. First, many people refer advisors because they like the advisor personally. They enjoy and trust the person. This is worth something, because people are more likely to act on advice given to them by someone that they like and trust. Unfortunately, many referrals are not based on an advisor's competence. Try to discern the quality of the referral when you get it. Why is this person being recommended? Is the advisor simply a really nice lady, or is she really sharp and up on the best and latest portfolio designs and solutions?

Second, many referrals made by professionals are not completely neutral. Frequently, a professional has a vested interest in steering you toward a particular advisor in exchange for compensation or future referrals. This may result in a recommendation that is based less on competence and more on economics. In many cases, this must be disclosed, but it often isn't.

While economics may result in a biased referral, however, a separate trend is pushing in the other direction. In today's litigious society, professionals and laypeople alike are less willing to refer you to others because of the implied endorsement that a referral provides. This is especially true for accountants and attorneys, who can be held liable for bad advice rendered by professionals that they refer. This makes it harder to get referrals, but it may result in a higher-quality referral when one is given. With these two trends pulling in opposite directions, you'll have to make a judgment call on the value of a professional referral.

If you're meeting an advisor who was referred, as always, go into the meeting with your eyes open. The referral is a great start, but you want to be sure that this person will be right for you and your needs. Go through all the areas we've covered to assess his potential as your advisor.

Referrals are probably most helpful if you have a specific need or approach, and you were referred by someone who is in a similar situation. If you are in or near retirement, someone who specializes in income planning can be a great referral. Yet be careful regarding the definition of a retirement specialist. While there are many experts who are well equipped to help you build a portfolio that generates income and growth while minimizing risk, there are also many others who interpret retirement as a euphemism for stepping off the planet. You may be retiring, but your life expectancy didn't suddenly drop to five years, and your ability to assume intelligent risk didn't disappear overnight. Putting all or most of your assets in guaranteed, low-interest accounts may seem safe, but it probably introduces unacceptable risk through future loss of purchasing power.

Similarly, if you are a doctor and another doctor whom you trust has an advisor who focuses on working with people in the medical community, the referral is more valuable simply because you may have found a specialist who is experienced in the issues that are important to you.

## List of Questions

When you are assessing a potential financial advisor, it may be helpful to have a basic list of questions drawn from the topics already covered. These questions provide a good starting point, and you can always add your own.

1. *What is your relevant experience as a financial professional?*
   You're looking for at least five years relevant experience, and hopefully significantly more.
2. *What is the profile of your typical client?*
   You're trying to be sure that her experience and the typical needs of her current clients match your individual needs.
3. *How would you describe your investment philosophy?*
   This is a broad question. Look for basic issues such as asset allocation, rebalancing your portfolio, controlling risk, and target investment return rates.
4. *What licenses do you hold?*
   Is the advisor dually licensed, or is he limited to selling only fee-based or only commission-based products and services?
5. *What is your experience with alternative investments, such as nontraded REITs, BDCs, oil and gas, commodities, and managed futures?*
6. *How do you charge for your services?*
   Fees are almost always the best option for traditional asset classes, while most alternatives are available only via a brokerage channel that must charge commissions. Most fee-based advisors charge around 1.00 percent per year of assets under management for their services. For larger accounts, you may be able to negotiate this down, but good advisors are worth their fees and often have little trouble finding clients who will pay them.

If you have gotten the answers you want from these questions, the rest serve primarily as confirmation.

1. *Do you use mutual funds?*
   The answer should be no. Possible exceptions could be a limited use of index funds, international funds, or funds offering access to unique investments. If the other answers were all the right ones,

but this one isn't, explore further. Few sophisticated advisors still use mutual funds liberally particularly for larger clients.

2. *How do you select and manage the different asset classes within a portfolio?*

   This is simply more confirmation that the advisor has systems in place to find and manage good third-party managers for the various asset classes you will be using. This can also help you assess the advisor's systems for keeping her emotions under control.

3. *What kind of special education, training, or certification have you received?*

   Certifications increase in importance if the advisor's experience is weak or difficult to discern. Otherwise, this may be of marginal or little importance.

4. *Do you have disciplinary problems on file with the FINRA or a state?*

   The answer should be no, but after the financial meltdown, investors filed many frivolous complaints that had little to do with the advisor's actions. If there are any, ask for a detailed explanation. If you're not comfortable with the answer, or if you don't understand it, ask to speak to the advisor's supervisor for a better explanation, or simply move on. Most problem advisors have a history of bad behavior.

5. *Can I speak with any of your other clients?*

   Be careful with this question. Ask it if you feel the need to check references and you really plan to follow up on a specific issue. Remember, it's relatively easy for an advisor to arrange for a friendly client to give a great recommendation regardless of his actual performance. Also, if an advisor is good and therefore is in demand, the interview will be a two-way street in which she will also be determining her desire to have you as a client. If you label yourself as difficult at the beginning of a potential relationship, you may be disqualified or referred elsewhere before you ever get started.

After running through these questions, you will have lots of information on the advisor's specific skills, and you should also have a pretty good idea of your comfort with him as a person. Expect to provide some meaningful data to the advisor so that he can decide if you're a good match for his services. A successful relationship needs to work for both you and your advisor.

## Partnering

You may be lucky and already know an excellent advisor with great experience, just the right expertise, and a practice focus that fits you perfectly. If so, congratulations! If not, these tips should help you dramatically narrow the field of advisors who can help you reach your financial goals.

The value of a good professional can be incredible, and advisors with strong expertise in advanced portfolio design and implementation can make financial success much more likely. Finding the right person may take a bit of effort, but unless you have the time, talent, and desire to manage your portfolio on your own, you need to find someone to help you take advantage of the incredible opportunities that are becoming available to individual investors, while also avoiding the problems that so many people routinely suffer on their own.

# 11

# The Best of Both Approaches

SOME PEOPLE WANT TO MANAGE AND CONTROL MUCH OF THEIR OWN investment portfolio, but recognize that an expert can provide them with valuable advice and access in some areas. You may love managing an individual stock portfolio, but still want the benefits of adding various alternatives to your portfolio. Access to a professional can also provide you with resources that may be difficult for you to find on your own, such as information on asset allocation, international investments, estate planning, tax issues, and life insurance. An advisor could offer you valuable assistance in these and other areas while you handle the parts of your portfolio that you like and enjoy managing.

Some investors may benefit from combining the best from the last two chapters. Probably the most common arrangement will leave you managing all or parts of the traditional assets in your portfolios and depending on a professional for access to and advice on diversification into alternatives. During the last few years, some investors have managed their stocks and bonds quite well, but enjoyed almost no success because of the market's dismal performance. Rather than turning over everything, professional advice may be best for only some assets.

Some of the financial professionals affiliated with my firm recognized that many individuals have this need and chose to specialize in alternatives. They leave the standard stocks and bonds to the individuals themselves or to one of the many, many other financial professionals that offer these services. They focus only on the much less crowded category of alternatives, and because they often introduce such different performance characteristics into a portfolio, their impact on portfolios is often disproportionately high. It's not necessarily because their recommendations are extraordinary, although they hopefully offer good advice. Their impact tends to be high because the diversification benefits are so much greater than those usually offered by more traditional performance assets, such as other subcategories of stocks.

This arrangement is not just for individual investors. It can also be great for professionals who specialize in other areas of finance, but recognize their limitations in investment planning and management. CPAs, life insurance specialists, and lawyers are good examples. CPAs are usually excellent at tax planning because they understand the ramifications of different actions. They also tend to be poor investors because they usually focus first on taxes and second on maximizing returns with acceptable risk. They may have very specific expertise with particular investments, such as oil and gas, but need help with the rest of their portfolios. Asset allocation strategies and stock market strategies have nothing to do with accounting, making CPAs great candidates for working with an advisor on a limited basis to address specific needs.

Beyond using a broker to gain access to alternatives, some people may also need some occasional financial advice. Many financial advisors, particularly fee-based advisors, offer assistance on an hourly basis.

Expect to pay a relatively high fee if you have no investments with an advisor and you want truly objective advice. Hourly rates of $200 to $400 or even higher are common. It may be difficult to pay out several hundred dollars for advice that may not clearly provide value now or in the future. Yet, the advisor's recommendations may pay

THE BEST OF BOTH APPROACHES

you back many, many times your cost through increased returns and avoided losses.

For many investors who are paying for advice on an hourly basis, the biggest challenge is continuing to seek the advice they need. It's easy to justify saving a few dollars by putting off or avoiding the appointment. The true costs, however, are often much higher if fee avoidance becomes the de facto strategy. If you follow this approach, you may want to develop a relationship with an advisor whom you meet with at least once a year. If you're going much longer than that between meetings and you're not an expert in multiple areas, you're probably missing opportunities or assuming risk that you don't want or understand.

Some investors also choose to diversify their financial advisors rather than working with only one or two. This can offer benefits, such as access to more information and expertise, but it also adds complexity, since investment strategies and investments must be coordinated across advisors and accounts.

The primary reason to use this approach is to leverage the strengths of different firms. You may have one advisor who specializes in domestic stocks and bonds, another who focuses on international holdings, and another with specific expertise in alternatives. This arrangement almost always requires clear understanding and strong conviction on the part of the investor because different advisors will often hold conflicting beliefs regarding the best portfolio design. Because they have chosen to focus on a particular area, they will usually believe strongly that a high percentage of your assets should be allocated to their specialty. Maintaining your optimum portfolio balance is likely to fall on your shoulders.

If you need income, juggling multiple advisors managing different assets can get messy. You will need to be actively involved in your accounts to be sure that income and liquidations come from the right assets at the optimum times.

Hopefully, your motivation for using multiple advisors springs from a desire to gain access to the best possible partners rather than a lack of trust in your current advisors. If you have a good advisor who is able to service all your needs competently, the benefits of more coordinated planning and implementation will probably offset the benefits of bringing another competing voice into decisions. If one person or firm provides all your advice, it should be easier for that person or firm to successfully advise you on your whole portfolio. Partly for this reason, a larger portfolio held in one place often makes fee negotiation easier as well.

One last tip: most people naturally compare their own performance to that of their professional if they outsource only part of the management, or they will compare the performance of different financial professionals to one another. This rarely makes sense, but it's easy to do.

The first decade of the century provides an easy illustration. If you hired one financial professional to manage your U.S. stocks, another for your international stocks, and a third for your alternatives, solid performance by all of them would probably have resulted in the alternatives manager clearly achieving the best performance, followed by your international manager, who was struggling with mid-single-digit annual returns. Your domestic stock manager probably would have had a pretty poor decade, as even negative annual returns would have put her at or near the top of the industry.

Many people would look at these numbers and assume that the alternatives manager did a great job while the domestic stock manager performed terribly. This could be true, but it's more likely that their respective performances resulted from their underlying markets. Even if the domestic stock manager outperformed her relevant benchmark by 3 to 5 percent per year, his or her fantastic performance still probably would have trailed mediocre management by professionals in other categories. In this case, the relative performance would have been great, even though the absolute performance remained terrible. I have seen many investors reward their poorest managers simply because their category did well and punish a good manager because of poor markets.

Any total portfolio strategy will be most effective when the respective managers most successfully execute the strategy you give them. With an endowment model allocation, different sectors will outperform others at different times. You're counting on this. When it inevitably happens, you also want to recognize that you want to reward good performance relative to particular markets, not relative to only the U.S. stock market.

Along the same lines, many investors give their financial professional the task of building a conservative stock portfolio while they play with a smaller amount of money on the side, usually in some version of an aggressive small-cap strategy. This can be lots of fun and help everyone stay more involved.

But many people fail to acknowledge the completely different risk profiles of the different approaches. If the market takes off and the individual investor's portfolio holds numerous high-risk positions that are likely to move much more than the market, some individuals become convinced that investing is easy because their portfolio went up, possibly much more than the more conservative manager's portfolio. During the late 1990s dot-com craze, countless investors fell into this trap. Their portfolios excelled, but only because their strategy's risk was extraordinarily high. Most people in this situation didn't understand how aggressive their portfolios were until after their stock accounts plummeted throughout 2000 to 2002.

If you outsource everything to one advisor, the advisor should manage various third-party managers for you. If you purposely utilize several different managers or manage parts of your portfolio in competition with your advisor, be sure you understand relative versus absolute performance and manage it well.

## 12

# Pulling It All Together

THE STRATEGIES AND INFORMATION COVERED THROUGHOUT THE
book should provide any investor with a great deal of practical information that can be used to create a much more advanced portfolio
than the traditional 60/40 stock/bond portfolio. As the industry
evolves to make more opportunities available to individual investors,
people with different portfolios and needs should all benefit from
strategies that include far more ways to participate in domestic and
international opportunities.

While these strategies can be adjusted to work for nearly any size
or type of investor, this last chapter will focus on investors who are
within five years of retirement. Since most people retire at around 65,
that would mean that these comments are generally targeted toward
someone in his sixties, but they are really most applicable to someone
who is nearing or just entering retirement. In fact, if you retire early,
many of these practices are probably even more applicable because
you are facing an even longer time frame with greater requirements
for your finances.

## Key Assumptions

More than in past years, your assumptions about your likely future and the future of global economies will probably affect your decisions. You may have ignored many of these issues in the past, but as you face key financial decisions, your perspective is likely to influence how you invest your assets. Your needs are more immediate, and you probably lack the time or the resources to rebuild your portfolio if you suffer severe losses.

Do you believe that the world is close to ending and that all your assets need to be protected via guarantees? Do you think we're going to experience rapid inflation that will severely erode the value of most fixed-interest-rate investments? Do you think that low valuations, exploding global growth, and rapidly changing access to investments opens up interesting possibilities in spite of global uncertainty? You may answer yes to all or none of these questions. Regardless, what is the best plan of action? Making just a few decisions should make all of this much easier.

If you are unwilling to assume any risk with your investments and are willing to accept annual returns of possibly well below 4 percent in spite of the threat of inflation, you are probably best off avoiding almost any type of investment. This makes your decisions easy. You can spread your assets over CDs, fixed-indexed annuities, or Treasury bonds. Your portfolio will face very little risk, but your assets will probably buy significantly less over time as inflation and taxes erode your purchasing power.

If you are more optimistic, you will probably want to assume some risk. Confidence in the future could result from low valuations, the increasing availability of cheap energy, rapidly growing global economies, and vastly expanded investment options through various means. I believe that all of these factors likely create an attractive investment environment in spite of the many challenges that U.S. investors clearly face. None of these events guarantees investment success, but together, they should make investment gains, particularly for individuals who are willing to include less traditional assets, much more attractive than they were in the lost decade following the turn of the century.

Assuming that you have some confidence in the future, another simple issue will be whether to diversify your assets beyond U.S. stocks and bonds. Adding international stocks has been easy for many years, and there seems to be little reason to avoid them. Adding international bonds may require a bit more expertise, since this asset class remains focused more on avoiding loss than on securing gains.

Your biggest decision will probably involve alternative assets. The success of endowments and institutions using these strategies provides a great road map, and rapidly escalating access to alternatives for individual investors makes emulating endowments much easier. I hope you will make the effort to take steps to dramatically alter your portfolio's performance and risk profile through adopting a more advanced portfolio design. When adding alternatives, most people start with nontraded REITs, followed by business development companies. After these basic additions, oil and gas tends to attract higher-net-worth individuals who are looking for tax incentives, while managed futures and commodities appeal to individuals who are seeking very strong diversification. People with larger portfolios often add private equity and possibly hedge funds.

Once you decide to include some risk assets and form a general opinion of alternatives, the next decision often centers on how many less risky assets versus more aggressive assets to include. Your income needs, discussed in Chapter 8, "Creating a Portfolio," will help with this decision. Ultra-low interest rates create the very strange circumstance that traditionally safe bonds and assets could be much riskier than assets that have been traditionally thought of higher risk. Only you can make a final decision on your comfort level, but keep in mind the increased risk of bonds and similar assets when interest rates are low and likely to increase.

You may have decided earlier that you want to work with a financial professional because you would rather avoid designing your own portfolio. That's fine, but I like to encourage every investor to develop some idea of his outlook on investments before he seeks assistance. Your general direction will affect whom you work with.

If you want only CDs, talk to banks. If you want guaranteed insurance products, find someone who specializes in annuities. If you believe that alternatives will make your portfolio stronger, you will need to find someone with expertise in this area. It helps to know at least a bit about your intended path before you start out.

You will want to make a specific decision on whether to manage your finances on your own or through a professional. You may already be working with someone who has been very helpful, and some of the concepts in the book may point out the value of an advisor with a different background and expertise. You may want to find someone new, or add another advisor with different expertise.

Part of your decision should include a very candid assessment of your ability to withstand the inevitable market ups and downs. Have you helped your portfolio perform better, or have you been part of the statistics cataloging the mismanagement of so many individual investors?

Answering just a few questions can help you move forward rapidly and get started in a profitable direction.

## Key Questions to Ask Yourself

1. Should I assume some risk in my portfolio? (Y/N)
2. Do I have some confidence in the future based on relatively low valuations, international growth, emerging trends such as the availability of inexpensive energy, or new access to diverse investments? (Y/N)
3. Do I need to change my investment approach with some or all of my traditional assets to avoid many of the performance problems and fees associated with mutual funds? (Y/N)
4. Do I want to adopt a portfolio strategy more similar to that of endowments and institutions, including the addition of diverse alternative asset classes? (Y/N)
5. Do I want to reduce my safer assets, such as fixed income, below the traditional 40 percent level because I believe my more

diversified performance assets will provide adequate income and diversification? (Y/N) If so, by how much?

6. Is my portfolio likely to perform better if a financial professional provides assistance with all or parts of my portfolio? (Y/N) If yes, which parts?

I hope that by this point, none of these decisions are difficult, and that you have enough information to quickly decide on your best plan of action. I am admittedly biased, but my experience and research tell me that most investors will benefit from assuming some portfolio risk, which can be lessened through incorporating highly diverse asset classes, including alternatives. It helps them build a portfolio with growth potential that also produces income with acceptable levels of risk. More advanced portfolio design can also result in decreased dependence on fixed income, which could experience very weak performance as we move through the twenty-first century and interest rates return to more normal levels.

Lastly, most people achieve greater investment success with the help of a good financial professional. It helps them make better decisions while providing access to far more resources and expertise.

Regardless, whether you implement everything in this book or pick and choose specific pieces, each step you take can help you excel and achieve greater financial success.

I hope you've enjoyed reading and learning from this as much as I enjoyed sharing some of my experience and strategies. I wish you the best in all your financial endeavors. May this book be a blessing to you and help you prosper.

If you are interested in building your own portfolio that follows the strategy outlined in the book, I invite you to experiment with software we've created that enables easy application of the book's concepts. The software helps you define estimates for returns and incomes from different investments, and then enables the quick creation of a portfolio that provides return and income estimates. You can also define the same inputs for your current portfolio and then compare your current portfolio to a portfolio based on the book's approach.

For more information, go to www.HowToKeepandGrow.com. For a special discount offered to readers of *How to Keep and Grow Your Retirement Assets*, use the code word "Howto." Again, best of luck!

# Notes

## From the Author

1. http://www.usatoday.com/money/industries/energy/story/2012-05-15/
   1A-COV-ENERGY-INDEPENDENCE/54977254/1.

## Chapter 1

1. MSCI (www.msci.com), www.msci.com/products/indices/country_and
   _regional/dm/.
2. ibid
3. ibid.
4. MSCI (www.msci.com), www.msci.com/products/indices/country_and
   _regional/em/.

## Chapter 2

1. DALBAR, Inc., "Quantitative Analysis of Investor Behavior (QAIB)," April
   2012, www.dalbar.com, www.qaib.com.
2. DALBAR, Inc., "Quantitative Analysis of Investor Behavior," January 1984–
   December 2000.
3. DALBAR, Inc., "Quantitative Analysis of Investor Behavior (QAIB)," 2001,
   www.dalbar.com www.qaib.com.
4. DALBAR, Inc., "Quantitative Analysis," April 2012.
5. David Brooks, *The Social Animal: The Hidden Sources of Love, Character, and
   Achievement* (New York: Random House, 2011), p. 167.
6. Indexes used are as follows: REITs: NAREIT All Equity REITs Index; EAFE:
   MSCI EAFE; oil: WTI Crude Index; bonds: Barclays Capital U.S. Aggregate
   Index; homes: median sale price of existing family home; gold: USD per troy
   ounce; inflation: CPI. Average asset allocation investor return is based on an
   analysis by DALBAR, Inc., that utilizes the net aggregate mutual fund sales,
   redemptions, and exchanges each month as a measure of investor behavior.
   Returns (and total return, where applicable) are annualized and represent the
   20-year period ending December 31, 2010, to match DALBAR's study.
7. *2012 Investment Company Fact Book*, 52nd Edition (Washington, DC:
   Investment Company Institute, 2012), p. 28.
8. Andrea Frazzini and Owen A. Lamont, "Dumb Money: Mutual Fund
   Flows and the Cross-Section of Stock Returns," Working Paper 11526,
   National Bureau of Economic Research, January 2005, p. 2, http://www
   .nber.org/papers/w11526.pdf.

9. DALBAR, "Quantitative Analysis," April 2012, p. 5.

10. http://www.dorseywrightmm.com/downloads/hrs_research/Point%20 and%20Figure%20Special%20Report.pdf.

## Chapter 3

1. H. M. Markowitz, "Portfolio Selection," *Journal of Finance* vol. 7, no. 1, March 1952, pp. 77–91. DOI:10.2307/2975974. JSTOR 2975974

2. The Yale Endowment Report for years 2000–2011, Harvard University Financial Report for years 2000–2011, and the Stanford Management Company Report for years 2000–2011. (Note: Endowments measure returns from July 1 through June 30.)

3. *2012 Investment Company Fact Book*, 52nd Edition (Washington, DC: Investment Company Institute, 2012), p. 86.

4. Ibid., p. 9.

5. Ibid., p. 11.

6. Ibid., p. 15.

7. Julie Creswell, "Mutual Funds Dirty Little Secrets," *Fortune*, September 1, 2003, http://money.cnn.com/magazines/fortune/fortune_ archive/2003/09/01/348192/index.htm.

8. "Mutual Funds, A Monthly Review, August 2005," *Wall Street Journal*, September 6, 2005, p. R1.

9. http://www.businessinsider.com/shocking-mutual-fund-statistics-2010-9?op=1.

10. Eric Tyson, "Star Funds Often Burn Out Quickly," *San Francisco Chronicle*, March 8, 1998, p. B-1.

11. http://www.forbes.com/sites/investor/2010/06/28/peter-lynch-wisdom-plus -10-stock-picks/.

12. Peter Lynch, *One Up on Wall Street* (New York: Simon and Schuster, Fireside Edition, 2000), p. 56.

13. *2012 Investment Company Fact Book*, p. 72.

14. John M. R. Chalmers, Roger M. Edelen, and Gregory B. Kadlec, "Mutual Fund Trading Costs," Rodney L. White Center for Financial Research, Wharton School, p. 4.

15. John Bogle, *Bogle on Mutual Funds* (New York: Dell Publishing, 1994), p. 173.

16. http://thefloat.typepad.com/the_float/2009/03/portfolio-turnover-and -transaction-costs.html.

17. Burton G. Malkiel, "Returns from Investing in Equity Mutual Funds 1971 to 1991," *Journal of Finance*, vol. 50, no. 2, June 1995.

18. Larry Swedro, "Survivorship Bias," April 13, 2001; originally published in *Journal of Finance*, March 1997.

19. Ibid.; originally published in *Wall Street Journal*, May 10, 1999.

20. Ibid.; originally published in *St. Louis Post-Dispatch*, February 7, 2000.

21. *2012 Investment Company Fact Book*, p. 15.

22. Swedro, "Survivorship Bias"; originally published in *Wall Street Journal*.

23. Karen Damato, "Mutual Fund Returns Are Different amid New Rules," *Wall Street Journal*, April 12, 2002, p. C1.

24. http://www.globaleconomicandinvestmentanalytics.com/archiveslist/ articles/727-why-investor-returns-are-so-bad.html.

25. Ibid.

## Chapter 4

1. http://seekingalpha.com/article/124295-s-p-p-e-ratio-is-low-but-has-been-lower.
2. http://seekingalpha.com/article/318256-s-p-500-p-e-mean-reversion-pick-your-poison-is-the-market-cheap-or-expensive.
3. http://observationsandnotes.blogspot.com/2011/01/start-pe-10-year-stock-market-return.html.
4. J.P. Morgan Asset Management, "Market Insights, 2Q 2011, Guide to the Markets," p. 22; Fidelity Investments, "Capital Markets Compendium," June 2012, p. 18.
5. Fareed Zakaria, Fidelity Investments Executive Forum, April 30, 2012.
6. *The Wall Street Journal*, The Market Driven Energy Revolution, Joel Kurtzman, Tuesday, May 22, 2012, p. A17.
7. http://www.inflationdata.com/inflation/inflation_rate/historicalinflation.aspx.
8. Ibid.
9. http://www.advisorperspectives.com/newsletters11/22-viceira3.php.
10. Bradford Cornell, "Economic Growth and Equity Investing," *Financial Analysts Journal, vol. 66, no. 1, January/February 2010, p. 63.*
11. http://www.cnbc.com/id/44261909/Is_High_Speed_Computer_Trading_Killing_Investing.
12. http://www.nytimes.com/2011/12/31/business/daily-stock-market-activity.html?pagewanted=all.
13. http://www.bloomberg.com/news/2011-12-15/wall-street-traders-confounded-as-global-volatility-extends-record-streak.html.
14. http://www.fedprimerate.com/wall_street_journal_prime_rate_history.htm; or David Frum, *How We Got Here: The '70s* (New York: Basic Books, 2000), pp. 292–293.
15. http://www.fedprimerate.com/.
16. Barclays website; or http://finance.yahoo.com/q?s=AGG.
17. http://www.treasury.gov/resource-center/data-chart-center/interest-rates/pages/textview.aspx?data=yield.
18. http://www.inflationdata.com/inflation/inflation_rate/historicalinflation.aspx.
19. http://bottomline.msnbc.msn.com/_news/2012/02/10/10372000-warren-buffett-bill-gross-spar-over-bond-investing?lite.

## Chapter 5

1. Peter Mladina and Jeffrey Coyle, "Yale Endowment Returns: Manager Returns or Risk Exposure?," *Journal of Wealth Management*, vol. 13, no. 1, Summer 2010, p. 47.
2. NACUBO (National Association of College and University Business Officers), "Dollar-Weighted Average Data from 842 Colleges and Universities," December 31, 2010.
3. Yale Endowment Report for 2011, Harvard University Financial Report for 2011, and Stanford Management Company Report for 2011. (Note: Endowments measure returns from July 1 through June 30.)
4. NACUBO, "Dollar-Weighted Average Data."

## Chapter 6

1. Fareed Zakaria, 2012 Fidelity Investments Executive Forum, April 29–May 2, 2012, Scottsdale, Arizona.
2. http://www.cato.org/zimbabwe.
3. Fama/French benchmark portfolios. In this analysis, growth stocks are defined as the bottom 30 percent of stocks traded on the NYSE ranked by book-to-market ratio, plus stocks traded on the AMEX and Nasdaq with equal or lower book-to-market ratios. Value stocks are defined as the upper 30 percent of stocks traded on the NYSE ranked by book-to-market ratio, plus stocks traded on the AMEX and Nasdaq with equal or higher book-to-market ratios. The median market capitalization of NYSE stocks is used as the breakpoint in classifying stocks as large or small. Index composition is determined in June and rebalanced annually.
4. Direxion, "Alternatives: How Much Is Enough?," August 9, 2012, p. 2. Distributed by Rafferty Capital Markets.
5. Virginia Munger Kahn, "Alternatives Becoming Mainstream," *Financial Advisor*, July 26, 2012; http://www.fa-mag.com/fa-news/11761-alternatives-becoming-mainstream.html.
6. "Non-Traded REIT Full-Cycle Performance Study," Executive Summary, The University of Texas at Austin, Real Estate Finance and Investment Center, and Blue Vault Partners, LLC, June 1, 2012, pp. 14, 15.
7. Harvard Management Company, "Endowment Report Message from the CEO," September 2011, p. 2.
8. The Yale Endowment Report 2010, p. 33.
9. Hedge Fund Research, "Investors Return to Hedge Fund Industry as New Model," press release, January 20, 2010.
10. Roger G. Ibbotson, Peng Chen, and Kevin X. Zhu, "The ABCs of Hedge Funds: Alphas, Betas, and Costs," *Financial Analysts Journal*, vol. 67, no. 1, 2011 p. 23.
11. Ibid., p. 18.

## Chapter 7

1. http://www.dogsofthedow.com.
2. www.dogsofthedow.com, www.msci.com
3. Roger G. Ibbotson, Peng Chen, and Kevin X. Zhu, "The ABCs of Hedge Funds: Alphas, Betas, and Costs," *Financial Analysts Journal*, vol. 67, no. 1, 2011, p. 21.

## Chapter 9

1. www.nareit.com; www.ncreif.com.
2. http://us.ishares.com/product_info/fund/performance/ICF.htm.

## Chapter 10

1. http://www.investmentnews.com/article/20120425/FREE/120429948.

# Index

# About the Author

**Daniel Wildermuth** is the founder and CEO of the investment brokerage firm Kalos Capital Inc. and the money management firm Kalos Management Inc., which represent over $1 billion in assets in 12,000-plus accounts across 50 offices managed by a staff of about 250. Kalos Capital provides comprehensive brokerage services including a vast offering of alternative investments, and Kalos Management offers multiple domestic and international equity and fixed-income strategies to financial professionals and individual clients. Mr. Wildermuth serves as Chief Investment Officer for Kalos Management.

His combined firms' average annual revenue growth over the past five years has exceeded 40 percent. Growth drivers include a national reputation and recognized expertise in training financial professionals how to implement the more advanced portfolio strategies covered in *How to Keep and Grow Your Retirement Assets*, and his earlier book, *Wise Money*.

He speaks frequently at industry conferences and events and is often quoted as an expert in the fields of alternative investments, the stock market, and the general economy.

Daniel continues to work directly with a small group of investors, and he has been awarded The FIVE STAR: Best in Client Satisfaction Wealth Manager Award every year of its existence.

Daniel and his firm have been profiled on CNBC and the Bravo television networks and, most recently, by *Forbes* magazine for the group's experience in working with advanced portfolio strategies for individual investors.

At his quarterly training programs he enables financial professionals from across the nation to better serve their clients through applying more advanced portfolio and money management solutions.

He serves as advisor for several different industry conferences, helping them to design and produce conferences best suited to financial professionals who are seeking to improve their individual practices.

For approximately two years, Mr. Wildermuth hosted the popular weekly radio show, *Money Talks with Daniel Wildermuth.*

Mr. Wildermuth earned an MBA in Finance from Anderson School at UCLA and an undergraduate degree in engineering from Stanford University. He graduated in the top 2 percent and 15 percent of classes, respectively.